THE PROPERTY INVESTORS MANAGEMENT HANDBOOK MANAGING RESIDENTIAL PROPERTY

DAVID WATSON

EDITOR: ROGER SPROSTON

Straightforward Guides
www.straightforwardbooks.co.uk

Straightforward Guides

© Straightforward Co Ltd 2024

All rights reserved. No part of this publication may be reproduced in a retrieval system or transmitted by any means, electronic or mechanical, photocopying or otherwise, without the prior permission of the copyright holders.

978-1-80236-347-0
Printed by
4edge www.4edge.co.uk

Cover design by BW Studio Derby

Whilst every effort has been made to ensure that the information contained within this book is correct at the time of going to press, the author and publisher can take no responsibility for errors or omissions contained within.

CONTENTS

Introduction   pp

Ch.1 Deciding to invest in Property-points to consider   13

Ch.2 Developing Your property Portfolio-Costs   20

Ch.3 Finding Suitable property -Buying a property   45

Ch.4 Buying a property at auction   57

Ch.5 Sourcing Suitable Tenants and Management   70

Ch.6 What should be provided under the tenancy   91

Ch.7 Knowing The law   97

Ch.8 Understanding Rent and Sources of Rent   107

Ch.9 Repairs and improvements   115

Ch.10 Houses in Multiple Occupation (HMO'S)   123

Ch.11 Taking back your property 137

Ch.12 Private tenancies in Scotland 145

Ch.13 Managing the finances-tax and other issues 169

Useful websites 180

Summary of terms 183

Index

Appendix 1-Landlords Checklist

****

INTRODUCTION

The aim of this revised edition of The Property Investors Management Handbook **(updated to 2024)** is to demonstrate in a clear and uncomplicated way the main considerations involved in developing and managing a residential property portfolio.

More stringent financial rules and prospective law changes are deterring an increasing number of landlords from investing in the private rental sector (indeed many are pulling out, seeing the opportunity for a decent return dwindling, exacerbated by falling property prices and rising mortgage costs. In addition, it is getting a lot harder for the would be landlord to gain access to the buy-to-let sector in various parts of the UK, in particular the southeast of England but also now in many other parts of the UK. because of continuing high prices,

Balanced against this, with rents across Britain set to rise by at least 20% over the next five years and with more and more individuals and families moving into the private rented sector, the opportunities for careful investment, considering financial and moral imperatives, are very much there.

However, a cautionary note here. The housing market in the UK is in a worse mess than ever (as is the case in many other parts of the world) a mess that has built up over a long period, driven by blind greed and short-sightedness.

Successive governments failed to see that housing security is necessary for both people and the economy, or more likely they put their heads in the sand.

So, a big question-if you intend to invest in property for profit, how can you conduct yourself in a way that does not exacerbate the problem? Should you invest for the long term to achieve the goal of a long term stable income whilst guaranteeing the security of the tenant with reasonable rents? Should you take care of your property, maintaining the value of the asset and, at the same time, ensuring that the tenants have a safe and secure environment? In the view of this writer the answer is yes on both counts.

Although it might be good for investors to receive high returns on their properties, the record rents inevitably mean hardship for many tenants. Hardship for many in a time of ongoing high inflation could mean a threat to rent flows in that tenants cease to pay rent.

Another factor is that property prices in many regions are starting to fall. So, ask yourself as a landlord or potential landlord: Why are you investing in property at such a time? Are you in it for the long term and can you weather a fall in property prices? Where are you going to invest? In short, what are your motivations for investing and do you know of the perils that might arise?

Having said all that, overall, private letting of residential property has grown significantly in the last 30 years. However, in some cases those who are involved in letting property do not have

Introduction

the professional knowledge needed to manage effectively and often end up in a mess. Little thought is given to the fact that a complex framework of law covers landlord and tenant, defining the relationship between the two. This is another reason for this book- to enlighten would be landlords when it comes to the laws.

We talked above about forthcoming legislation which will greatly affect landlords as they manage their properties. Below is the government's summary of the Renters Reform Bill, currently on hold due to the general election (at the time of writing June 2024).

The Renters Reform Bill 2023

The Renters (Reform) Bill, although shelved due to the impending election, is still alive and active and it is hoped will see the light of day as an Act by the incoming government. The eventual Act will deliver on the government's commitment to "bring in a better deal for renters", including abolishing 'no fault' evictions and reforming landlord possession grounds. It will legislate for reforms set out in the private rented sector white paper published in June 2022.

Background

A healthy private rented sector is a vital part of our housing market – providing much-needed flexibility and in many cases serving as a steppingstone towards home ownership. The overall number of privately rented properties has doubled since 2004 – peaking in

2016 and remaining roughly stable since. For the most part, the sector works well for both landlords and tenants. However, some renters face a precarious lack of security as a result of section 21 'no fault' evictions.

Short notice moves worsen children's educational outcomes, make it challenging to hold down stable employment, and prevent families putting down roots and investing in their local area.

Nearly a quarter of private rented homes do not meet basic decency standards. The tragic death of two-year-old Awaab Ishak shone a light on the unacceptable state of this damp, cold and dangerous housing – but these problems are not limited to the social rented sector. The government intends to tackle these issues in the private rented sector by legislating to apply a Decent Homes Standard. These dilapidated homes are costing the NHS an estimated £340 million per annum and are holding back local areas, making them less attractive places to live and work.

Responsible landlords face challenges too – including when evicting tenants who willfully do not pay rent or exhibit anti-social behavior. They also suffer by being undercut by a minority of criminal landlords. Reforms aim to celebrate the overwhelming majority of landlords who do a good job and give them peace of mind that they can repossess their property when a tenant is behaving badly, or their circumstances change.

Introduction

Overview of Bill measures

The Renters (Reform) Bill will improve the system for both the 11 million private renters and 2.3 million landlords in England. The reforms have been developed in consultation with landlord and tenant groups over the past 5 years. The Renters (Reform) Bill will:

- Abolish section 21 'no fault' evictions and move to a simpler tenancy structure where all assured tenancies are periodic – providing more security for tenants and empowering them to challenge poor practice and unfair rent increases without fear of eviction;
- Introduce more comprehensive possession grounds so landlords can still recover their property (including where they wish to sell their property or move in close family) and to make it easier to repossess properties where tenants are at fault, for example in cases of anti-social behavior and repeat rent arrears;
- Provide stronger protections against backdoor eviction by ensuring tenants can appeal excessively above-market rents which are purely designed to force them out. As now, landlords will still be able to increase rents to market price for their properties and an independent tribunal will make a judgement on this, if needed. To avoid fettering the freedom of the judiciary, the tribunal will continue to be able to determine the actual market rent of a property;

- Introduce a new Private Rented Sector Ombudsman which will provide fair, impartial, and binding resolution to many issues and prove quicker, cheaper, and less adversarial than the court system;
- Create a Privately Rented Property Portal to help landlords understand their legal obligations and demonstrate compliance (giving good landlords confidence in their position), alongside providing better information to tenants to make informed decisions when entering into a tenancy agreement. It will also support local councils – helping them target enforcement activity where it is needed most; and
- Give tenants the right to request a pet in the property, which the landlord must consider and cannot unreasonably refuse. To support this, landlords will be able to require pet insurance to cover any damage to their property.

Further improvements to the private rented sector

Alongside the Renters (Reform) Bill, the government is working in partnership with the Ministry of Justice and HM Courts and Tribunals Service, to ensure that, in the small proportion of tenancies where court action is required, court users can use a modern, digital service. This remains a priority for the government. Following the recommendation of the Levelling Up, Housing and Communities Select Committee, we will align the abolition of

Introduction

section 21 and new possession grounds with court improvements. This includes end-to-end digitisation of the process and our work with the courts to explore the prioritisation of certain cases, including anti-social behavior.

The private rented sector white paper also committed to further reforms to support both landlords and tenants. The government remains fully committed to implementing these reforms and will bring forward legislation at the earliest opportunity to:

- Apply the Decent Homes Standard to the private rented sector to give renters safer, better value homes and remove the blight of poor-quality homes in local communities. This will help deliver the government's Levelling Up mission to halve the number of non-decent rented homes by 2030. The government launched a consultation in September 2022 to ensure the Decent Homes Standard is applied and enforced appropriately and fairly in the private rented sector. The government will respond to this and set out the next steps in due course;
- Make it illegal for landlords and agents to have blanket bans on renting to tenants in receipt of benefits or with children – ensuring no family is unjustly discriminated against when looking for a place to live; and

- Strengthen local councils' enforcement powers and introduce a new requirement for councils to report on enforcement activity – to help target criminal landlords.
- For more information about the Bill go to: www.gov.uk/guidance/guide-to-the-renters-reform-bill

****

CHAPTER ONE

DECIDING TO INVEST IN PROPERTY-GENERAL POINTS TO CONSIDER

Investing in Property

Notwithstanding all that has been said in the introduction, the overall demand for private rented property is now stronger than ever, with the mortgage market restricted for purchasers and house price inflation, particularly in the southeast, but increasingly through many areas of the UK, creating the need for high deposits which people cannot find. Essentially, accessing finance has become a big issue. The banks favor those with large cash deposits. This is the same in the buy-to-let sector as it is for domestic mortgages.

However, if finance can be arranged then the yields that one can expect from buy-to-let properties are high by comparison, currently standing at 6% on average. Of course, this depends on where the property is located. See overleaf for tables indicating the best and worst buy to let areas in the UK.

A yield is a portfolio's annual rental income as a percentage of total value. Because demand for private rented property is high, particularly as first-time buyers cannot get a toehold in the market, they are instead turning to the private rental sector, where rents are increasing. Therefore, investing in property for the longer term, as opposed to investing for short-term gain, is still a viable option.

Best and worst buy-to-let areas in the UK.

The graph below gives some idea of the current regional variations in rents and rental yields in the UK. Unsurprisingly the Southeast fares the worst whilst northern areas are the best when considering purchasing property. It is the case that many landlords and would-be landlords prefer to invest nearer to home so that they can retain more control over properties and keep management costs down, thus increasing profits.

REGION	AVERAGE PROPERTY PRICE	5-YR PRICE CHANGE	AVERAGE MONTHLY RENT	AVERAGE RENTAL YIELD
Scotland	£206,649	23.51%	£922	5.70%
Northeast	£227,892	20.71 %	£782	4.72%
Wales	£265,444	36.62 %	£919	4.68 %
Northwest	£239.021	28.48 %	£821	4.38 %
West Midlands	£299.281	28.03 %	£923	4.11 %
East Midlands	£250,552	27.45 %	£790	4.10 %

Greater London	£597,917	14.47 %	£1,914	4.00 %
Southeast	£456,964	21.65 %	£1, 351	3.80 %
Southwest	£378,791	28.51 %	£1,121	3.78 %
East of England	£408,430	22.09 %	£1.189	3.65 %

Rental yields

Investment properties which are rented out receive an income from tenants. To calculate the gross rental yield the annual rental income is divided by the purchase price of the property (annual rent÷price) X 100 = Gross rental yield). So, if the property was purchased for £75,000 (total) and the rent received is £450 per month the yield would be £5400 (annual rent) ÷ £75,000 X 100 which equals an annual yield of 7.2. This is a very respectable return on your capital. Of course, if you are a landlord then you will want to factor in the costs of being a landlord, such as maintenance, insurance, loan costs, empty periods etc.

Capital yields

When a property increases with time, this is known as capital growth. A simple example is if you buy a property for £75,000 and it increases by 25% there will be a capital appreciation of £18,750. It is a rule of thumb that low price properties might produce a high rental yield and low capital growth and vice-versa, although this is not always the case. Again, each case differs, and many factors will play a part but as long as you know what you want then you should be safe with your investment.

As with everything, property is a good investment if it is managed well. Too many would-be landlords buy property and neglect it which has a negative impact on the environment and a negative impact on the investment. A run-down property will decrease in value and the possibility of renting it out for a full market rent will also diminish. That is what this book is all about-how to become a good landlord and a good property manager and how to maximize the returns on your property.

What kind of property is suitable for letting?

Obviously, there are several different markets when it comes to people who rent. There are those who are less affluent, young, and single, in need of a sharing situation, but more likely to require more intensive management than older more mature (perhaps professional) people who can afford a higher rent but require more for their money.

The type of property you have, its location, its condition, will very much determine the rent levels that you can charge and the clients that you will attract. The type of rent that a landlord might expect to achieve will be percentage of the value of the freehold of the property, (or long leasehold in the case of flats). The eventual profit will be determined by the level of any existing mortgage and other outgoings. If you are renting out a flat, it could be that it is in a mansion block or other flatted block and the service charge will need to be added to the rent. When letting a property, it is necessary to consider profit after mortgage payments and likely tax bill plus other outgoings such as insurance and agents fees (if any).

Of course, there are other factors which make the profit achieved less important, that is the capital growth of the property. See further on in the book for a breakdown of taxation and allowances.

The importance of having a clear business plan

As a (would be) private landlord, a person considering letting a property for profit, or already doing so, it is vital that you are very clear about the following:

- What kind of approach do you intend to take as a landlord? Do you intend to purchase, or do you have, an up-market property which you are going to rent out to stable professional tenants who will pay their rent on time and look after the property (hopefully)
- What are the key factors that affect the value of a property in rental terms? Is the property close to public transport, does it have a garden, what floor is it on and what size are the rooms? Is it secure and in a crime free area? If you are acquiring a

property, you should set out what it is you are trying to achieve in the longer term, i.e., the type of person you want and match this to the likely residential requirements of that hypothetical person. You can then gain an idea of what type of property you
- are looking for, in what area, and you can then see whether you can afford such a property. If not, you may have to change your plan.
- Do you intend to let to young single people, perhaps students, who will occupy individual rooms achieving higher returns but causing potentially greater headaches? Are you aware of the headaches? It is vitally important that you understand the ramifications of letting to different client groups and the potential problems in the future.
- Are you clear about the impact on the environment, and to other people, that your activities as a landlord may have? For example, do you have a maintenance plan which ensures that not only does your property look nice and remain well maintained but also considers whether the plan, or lack of it, will have an impact on the rest of the neighborhood? Will the type of tenant you intend to attract affect the rest of those living in the immediate vicinity?
- What are the aims and objectives underpinning your business plan? Do you have a business plan or are you operating in an unstructured way? Considering the above, it is obviously

Deciding to Invest in Property-Points to Consider

necessary that you have a clear picture of the business environment that you intend to operate in, the legal and economic framework that governs and regulates the environment.

- It is vital that you are very clear about what it is you are trying to achieve. You should either understand the type of property that you already own or have an idea of the property you are trying to acquire to fit what client group. These goals should be very clear in your own mind and based on a long-term projection, underpinned by knowledge of the law and economics of letting property.
- As an exercise you should sit down and map out your business plan before you go any further. Whether you are an existing property owner or wish to acquire a property for the purpose of letting, the first objective is to formulate a business plan.

****

CHAPTER 2

DEVELOPING YOUR PROPERTY PORTFOLIO-COST CONSIDERATIONS

Budget

Before beginning to look for a house or flat for investment you need to sit down and give careful thought to the costs.

Deposit

Sometimes the estate agent (if you are buying through an estate agent) will ask you for a small deposit when you make the offer. This indicates that you are serious about the offer and is a widespread and legitimate practice if the deposit is not too much. £100 is usual. However, this practice can vary. In London for example deposits can be quite a lot higher.

The main deposit for the property, i.e., the difference between the mortgage and what has been accepted for the property, isn't paid until the exchange of contracts. Once you have exchanged contracts on a property the purchase is legally binding. Until then, you are free to withdraw. The deposit cannot be reclaimed after exchange. Banks will normally lend up to 75 percent of the purchase price of the property for buy-to-let.

However, the less you borrow the more favorable terms you can normally get from a bank or building society. This particularly applies now, with the tightening of lending criteria.

Buy-to-Let Mortgages

Buy-to-let (BTL) mortgages are for landlords who buy property to rent out. The rules around buy-to-let mortgages are like those around regular mortgages, but there are some key differences.

Who can get a buy-to-let mortgage?

You can get a buy-to-let mortgage if:

- You want to invest in houses or flats.
- You can afford to take a risk. Investing in property is risky, so you shouldn't take out a BTL mortgage if you can't afford to take that risk.
- You already own your own home. You'll struggle to get a buy-to-let mortgage if you don't already own your own home, whether outright or with an outstanding mortgage.
- You have a good credit record and aren't stretched too much on your other borrowings such as your existing mortgage and credit cards.

- You earn £25,000+ a year. Otherwise, you might struggle to get a lender to approve your buy-to-let mortgage.
- You're under a certain age. Lenders have upper age limits, typically between 70 or 75. This is the oldest you can be when the mortgage ends not when it starts. For example, if you are 45 when you take out a 25-year mortgage it will finish when you're 70. However, these limits change all the time, so you need to check out a range of lenders.

How do buy-to-let mortgages work?

Buy-to-let mortgages are a lot like ordinary mortgages, but with some key differences:
- Interest rates on buy-to-let mortgages are usually higher.
- The fees also tend to be much higher.
- The minimum deposit for a buy-to-let mortgage is usually 25% of the property's value (although it can vary between 20-40%).
- Many BTL mortgages are interest-only. This means you don't pay anything each month, but at the end of the mortgage term you repay the capital in full.
- A significant proportion of BTL mortgage lending is not regulated by the Financial Conduct Authority (FCA).
- There are exceptions, for example, if you wish to let the property to a close family member (e.g., spouse, civil partner, child, grandparent, parent, or sibling). These are often referred

to as consumer buy-to-let mortgages and are assessed according to the same strict affordability rules as a residential mortgage.

How much you can you borrow for buy-to-let mortgages

The maximum you can borrow is linked to the amount of rental income you expect to receive. Lenders typically need the rental income to be 25–30% higher than your mortgage payment. To find out what your rent might be, talk to local letting agents or check the local press and online to find out how much similar properties are rented for.

Where to get a buy-to-let mortgage

Most of the big banks and some specialist lenders offer BTL mortgages. It's a good idea to talk to a mortgage broker before you take out a buy-to-let mortgage, as they will help you choose the most suitable deal for you.

Using price comparison websites

Comparison websites are a good starting point for anyone trying to find a mortgage tailored to their needs. The following are the most popular: Moneyfacts, Money Saving Expert, MoneySuperMarket, Which? Comparison websites won't all give you the same results, so make sure you use more than one site before deciding. It is also important to do some research into the type of product and features you need before making a purchase or changing supplier. Don't assume that your property will always have tenants. There will almost certainly be 'voids' when the property is unoccupied, or rent isn't paid, and you'll need to have a financial 'cushion' to meet your mortgage payments. When you do have rent coming in, use some of it to top up your savings account.

You might also need savings for major repair bills. For example, the boiler might break down, or there may be a blocked drain.

Stamp duty for Buy-to-Let properties
Stamp Duty Land Tax (SDLT) for buy to let properties is an extra 3% on top of the current SDLT rate bands. If you're purchasing a buy-to-let property or a second home in the UK, you'll need to pay a stamp duty land tax surcharge. The stamp duty land tax (SDLT) surcharge on second homes is an additional 3% on top of the regular residential stamp duty rate you would pay. However, as is usual with taxes, there are certain rules and exemptions that apply.

For more detailed information concerning SDLT for Buy to let properties go to www.gov.uk/stamp-duty-land-tax/residential-property-rates.

See table overleaf.

Developing Your Property Portfolio-Cost Considerations

Property or lease premium or transfer value	SDLT rate
Up to £250,000 (£425,00 first time buyers)	Zero
The next £675,000 (the portion from £250,001 to £925,000)	5%
The next £575,000 (the portion from £925,001 to £1.5 million)	10%

Property or lease premium or transfer value	SDLT rate
The remaining amount (the portion above £1.5 million)	12%

When do I need to pay the SDLT surcharge?

You are required to pay the surcharge 30 days after the completion of the sale, normally paid at the same time you would pay the SDLT.

Stamp duty surcharge for overseas buyers

Since April 2021, overseas-based buyers of residential properties in England and Northern Ireland have been required to pay a surcharge of 2% on top of the normal rates. This applies on top of the 3% buy-to-let surcharge - so overseas residents buying an investment property will need to pay stamp duty at 5% more than the standard rates for UK home movers.

What if the home I am buying replaces my main residence?

If the property you are buying replaces your main residence, you will not be liable for the 3% surcharge, even if you already own an additional property at the time of purchase. However, you must demonstrate that the main residence will be sold or gifted away – if you own it.

What if I'm a first-time buyer?

If you don't already own any property and are looking to invest in a buy-to-let, then you won't pay the additional stamp duty rate as you will only own one property. Note that you will not qualify for first-time buyer stamp duty relief as it can only be used for a property you intend to live in.

Other costs

A solicitor normally carries out conveyancing of property. However, individuals can do their own conveyancing, although it isn't as simple as it appears.

All the necessary paperwork can be obtained from legal stationers, and it is executed on a step-by-step basis. It must be said that solicitors are now very competitive with their charges and, for the sake of between £850-£1500 including VAT, it is better to let someone else do the work which allows you to concentrate on other things. Another issue will be that your lender will not look favorably on you doing your own conveyancing and will usually insist on the use of a solicitor or licensed conveyancer.

Land Registry

The Land Registry records all purchases of land in England and Wales and is open to the public (inspection of records, called a property search).

The registered title to any piece of land or property will carry with it a description and include the name of the owner, mortgage, rights over other person's land and any other rights. There is a small charge for inspection. A lot of solicitors have direct links and can carry out searches very quickly. Not all properties are registered although it is now a duty to register all transactions.

Capital Gains Tax on buy to let property

If you sell a property in the UK, you might need to pay capital gains tax (CGT) on the profits you make.

You generally won't need to pay tax when selling your main home.

However, you will usually face a CGT bill when selling a buy-to-let property or second home. You may also need to pay CGT if your home is partly used as business premises, or if you lease out part of your property.

CGT rates on property

In the UK, you pay higher rates of CGT on property than other assets.

Basic-rate taxpayers pay 18% on gains they make when selling property, while higher and additional-rate taxpayers pay 28%.

With other assets, such as shares, the basic-rate of CGT is 10%, and the higher-rate is 20%.

Bear in mind that any capital gains will be added to your other income sources when working out which income tax bracket you'll fall into for the year, and therefore might push you into a higher bracket.

All taxpayers have an annual CGT allowance, meaning they can earn a certain amount tax-free.

In 2024-25 you can make tax-free capital gains of up to £3000 - down from £6,000 in 2023-24. .

Couples who jointly own assets can combine this allowance, potentially allowing a gain of £6,000 without paying any tax.

You're not allowed to carry over any unused CGT allowance into the next tax year - so if you don't use it, you'll lose it.

How much CGT will I pay?

As the name suggests, CGT is only charged on the gains you make (the profit), rather than the full amount you sell the property for.

To work out your gain, you can deduct the amount you originally paid for the property from the sales price.

You can also deduct any legitimate costs involved with buying and selling the property. This includes things like broker fees, stamp duty, and some improvements to the property that were made while you owned it.

You can also offset losses you've made when selling other assets. For instance, if you own several properties and make, say, a £50,000 loss when selling one of them, you can use that against the gains you make from another property and therefore reduce your overall CGT bill. You should claim any losses on your self-assessment tax return, or by calling HMRC. You can claim losses for up to four years after they were incurred.

For any taxable gains above the tax-free allowance of £3,000 in 2024-25 you'll pay the CGT property rates.

When is capital gains tax on property due?

For UK properties sold on or after 27 October 2021, you must pay the tax owed within 60 days of the completion of the sale or disposal.

You'll do this by submitting a 'residential property return' and making a payment on account.

For property sales made between 6 April 2020 and 26 October 2021, the window to pay your CGT bill was 30 days.

What can I deduct from my taxable gain?

You're allowed to deduct certain costs from your gain if they're involved with buying and selling the property. These include:

- solicitor and estate agent fees

- stamp duty when buying the property.

Costs involved with improving the property, such as paying for an extension, can also be taken into account when working out your taxable gain.

However, you're not allowed to deduct costs involved with the upkeep of a property. You're not allowed to deduct mortgage interest either (though that can reduce the tax you pay on rental income).

Example of selling a second home

Someone is selling a second home in England in 2024-25 for £220,000 after buying it 10 years ago for £120,000. Their capital gain is the increase in the property value, which is £100,000.

However, they spent £5,000 on solicitor fees and estate agent fees when selling the property, which reduces their gain to £95,000. They have no other gains or losses, so they can simply use their £3,000 CGT allowance - reducing the taxable part of their gain to £92,000.

The rate of CGT they'll pay depends on their other income. In this case, let's say it's £25,000.

This means they'd pay 18% basic-rate CGT on £25,270 of their gain (taking them up to the threshold of £50,270) - coming in at

£4,548.60. They'd have to pay the higher rate of 28% on the remaining £63,730, which is £17,844.40. Altogether, the CGT bill would be £22,393.

Capital gains tax and your main home

You don't have to pay CGT on the sale of your main home.

That said, you may have a capital gains tax bill to pay if you:

- develop your home, for example, by converting part of it into flats
- sell part of your garden, and your total plot - including the area you're selling - is more than half a hectare (1.2 acres)
- use part of your home exclusively for business
- let out all or part of your home - this doesn't include having a single lodger if you are living in the property, too
- moved out of your property nine months or more ago - to move into a partner's home, for example
- bought a home for the purpose of renovating it and selling it on.

Which property is my main home?

If you use more than one home, you can nominate which will be tax-free for CGT purposes. It doesn't have to be the one where you live most of the time.

Developing Your Property Portfolio-Cost Considerations

Generally, it makes sense to nominate the property that's you expect to make the largest gain when you come to sell it. You have two years from when you get a new home to make the nomination. Married couples and civil partners can have only one main home between them, but unmarried couples can each nominate a different home.

Remember, you don't get tax relief if you bought your home just to sell it on and make a gain.

How does letting relief work with CGT?
If you have let out either all or part of a property, a proportion of any gain when you sell it could be taxable. But if you used to live in the property (or still did at the time of selling), you might be able to claim letting relief, which will reduce your capital gains tax bill.

Letting relief doesn't apply to buy-to-let investors who let out their properties and never live in them, and it's now only available for people who have been in shared occupancy with their tenant/tenants. You can also only claim relief on the proportion of the property being let for the period of time it was let out for.

The amount of letting relief you can claim will be the lowest of either the gain you receive from the letting proportion of the home, or the amount of private residence relief you can claim, or £40,000.

Note that you can't claim private residence relief and letting relief for the same period. So, if you are letting the property out when you sell it, the past nine months of ownership will qualify for private residence relief rather than letting relief.

The exact amount of private residence relief and letting relief you can get depends on the amount you sell the home for.

However, it may change things in terms of CGT. If you sell the property, the CGT you owe will be based on the increase in value between the date you were given the property - not the date of their death - and the date you sell it.

This is the case even though there may also be inheritance tax to pay on the home at the time of death.

Energy performance certificates for Buy-to-Let properties

From 1st April 2020, landlords must ensure the Energy Performance Certificates for their properties meet a new standard. This is for new and existing tenancies.

On 1st April 2018, it became a legal requirement for residential landlords to ensure their Energy Performance Certificates (EPCs) have a minimum rating of E. The regulations initially only applied for a new tenancy to a new tenant and a new tenancy to an existing tenant. Now, this law has been extended.

An EPC is needed whenever a property is built, sold, or rented. All landlords must order an Energy Performance Certificate for potential buyers or tenants before marketing their properties to sell or let.

What does an EPC contain?

An EPC includes information about a property's energy use and typical energy costs. It also contains recommendations about how to reduce energy usage and save money. It assigns the property an energy efficiency rating from A (most efficient) to G (least efficient). This is valid for ten years.

How do I get an Energy Performance Certificate?

You must find an accredited assessor to evaluate your property and produce the certificate. Landlords with properties in England, Wales and Northern Ireland should go to:
https://www.epcregister.com/searchAssessor.html

Those with properties in Scotland can find an assessor here: https://www.scottishepcregister.org.uk/assessorsearch

When is an Energy Performance Certificate required?

EPCs are required as follows for these dwellings:

- **Individual house/dwelling** (e.g., a self-contained property with its own kitchen/bathroom facilities) In this instance, one EPC is required for the dwelling.
- **Self-contained flats** (e.g., each behind its own front door with its own kitchen/bathroom facilities)-One EPC per flat will be needed.

- **Bedsits or room lets where there is a shared kitchen, toilet and/or bathroom** (e.g., a property where each room has its own tenancy agreement)-No EPC is required.
- **Shared flats/houses** (e.g., letting of a whole flat or house to students/young professionals etc. on a single tenancy agreement)-One EPC for the whole house is required.
- **Mixed self-contained and non-self-contained accommodation-**One EPC for each self-contained flat/unit, but no EPC for the remainder of the property.
- A room in a hall of residence or hostel-No EPC is required.

Energy Performance Certificates and Section 21 notices

As of 1st October 2015, landlords must provide an EPC to tenants before issuing a Section 21 notice to evict them. Legislation states that an EPC must be given to the person who becomes the tenant. This must be free of charge.

Tenants' rights to request energy efficiency improvements

As of 1st April 2016, tenants can request consent from their landlords to conduct energy efficiency improvements in their properties. The landlord cannot unreasonably refuse content.

However, it's the responsibility of the tenant to ensure that the works are funded. The intention is that no upfront costs should fall on the landlord unless the landlord wishes to contribute.

Future minimum energy efficiency standards in the UK
- From 1st April 2023, it is a legal requirement for all let properties to meet this standard. This is even if a tenancy agreement is already in place and includes both domestic and non-domestic lets.
- From 2028, it is believed that the minimum requirement will be raised to C.

How much will it cost to upgrade to C?
Inevitably, upgrading an E-rated property to meet the proposed C-rated standard will come with a heftier price tag than it would for a D-rated home. But landlords should expect the Government to cap the required amount of spending.

Government proposals include a £10,000 cap on the maximum spend per property – regardless of whether or not the C rating is achieved. Landlords of higher value properties face paying more, as it is understood that this cap could now work on a sliding scale, starting at £5,000, and rising in line with the rental value of the property.

But most landlords would spend far less than this on energy-efficiency measures, suggesting expensive investments such as heat pumps and solar panels will not be required.

The Energy Savings Trust, a charity, said the easiest way to insulate a property cheaply is to properly insulate it. It can be hard to gauge the quality of a property's pre-existing insulation, but Octopus Energy, a provider, has been known to loan out thermal cameras which can make the process a little easier.

According to the EST, a quarter of heat is lost through the roof in an uninsulated home.

"Installed correctly, loft insulation should pay for itself many times over in its 40-year lifetime," it says.

The charity estimates that insulating the loft of a typical semi-detached house costs around £640 in 2023 and would save £335 a year in energy bills.

The insulation a house might require depends on when it was built; it is considerably more expensive for older homes. Those built after the 1920s typically have cavity walls, which cost around £1,000 to insulate. This can bring big savings: a semi-detached home will make back £395 a year, the EST calculates.

Solid walls, more common in older houses, cost about £12,000 to insulate externally and £8,500 to insulate internally, excluding redecorating costs. Floor insulation is between £1,600 and £2,900 for a typical "suspended" floor.

However, costs can be trimmed by sourcing cheaper materials. Savvy landlords can salvage insulation from local building works that would otherwise end up in a skip using online marketplaces such as Facebook or Gumtree. Some are slashing their maintenance costs by 25pc by collecting building materials that would otherwise end up in a skip.

Apps have been developed for this very purpose, such as Sustainability Yard, where materials being traded are up to 80pc cheaper than they are new, while 30pc are free.

Do I need to buy a heat pump or solar panels for my rental property?

While the Government is pushing to meet certain net zero targets by 2050, which includes a target to install 600,000 heat pumps a year by 2028, buy-to-let landlords need not worry about installing if their only goal is to upgrade their EPC to a C-rating.

If anything, doing so could have the opposite effect: the current grading system is based on bills, not on carbon output, meaning it can punish people for installing heat pumps and it incentivizes the use of gas over electricity.

Inconsistencies in the system mean that homeowners can pay thousands of pounds for work that they later find actually lowered their EPC rating.

In the coming decades, landlords will have no choice in the matter, however. From 2035, homeowners will no longer be permitted to replace gas boilers like-for-like, making heat pump installations all but mandatory, but that does not mean it will be illegal to have one that was installed before that date.

Until 2025, households can claim a £5,000 grant to help with the cost of installing a heat pump, which typically exceeds £10,000. But if your only goal is to achieve a C-rated EPC, expensive green technology is not necessary. The same is true for solar panels, which cost £5,500 on average, according to the EST, depending on the type of panel, the size of the area covered and any difficulties with access to the roof. But for a buy-to-let landlord's purposes, they do not justify their investment if your only aim is to improve efficiency.

General exemptions

It is illegal to let property that breaches this EPC requirement. Upgrades must be made to improve the rating unless there is an applicable exemption.

This includes the following circumstances:
- Such work would devalue the property by 5% or more
- Recommended work has been carried out, but the rating did not improve

- The mortgage lender will not approve the recommended upgrades
- The building is listed, and the upgrades would 'unacceptably alter' property's character or appearance

If you believe your let falls into one of these categories, you can register it on the PRS Exemptions Register.

Penalties for non-compliance
If you fail to meet these regulations, a fine of up to £5,000 could be imposed for any breaches.

Structural surveys
The basic structural survey is the homebuyers' survey and valuation, which is normally carried out by the building society or other lender, and it will cost you between £200-350 and is not really an in-depth survey, merely allowing the lender to see whether they should lend or not and how much they should lend.

Sometimes lenders keep what they refer to as a retention, which means that they will not forward the full value (less deposit) until certain defined works have been carried out.

If you want to go further than a homebuyer's report, then you will have to instruct a firm of surveyors who have several survey types, depending on how far you want to go and how much you want to spend. A word of caution: many people go rushing headlong into buying a flat or house. If you stop and think about this, it is complete folly and can prove very expensive later. A house or flat is a commodity like other commodities, except that it is usually a lot more expensive. A lot can be wrong with the commodity that you have purchased which is not immediately obvious. Only after you have completed the deal and paid over the odds for your purchase do you begin to regret what you have done. The true market price of a property is not what the estate agent is asking, certainly not what the seller is asking. The true market price is the difference between what a property like one in good condition is being sold at and your property minus cost of works to bring it up to that value. Therefore, if you have any doubts whatsoever, and if you can afford it, get a detailed survey of the property you are proposing to buy and get the works that are required costed out.

When negotiating, this survey is an essential tool to arrive at an accurate and fair price. Do not rest faith in others, particularly when you alone stand to lose.

One further word of caution. As stated, a lot of problems with property cannot be seen. A structural survey will highlight those. In some cases, it may not be wise to proceed at all.

Mortgage arrangement fees

Depending upon the type of mortgage you are considering you may have to pay an arrangement fee. You should budget for anything up to 2% of the purchase price.

****

CHAPTER 3

FINDING SUITABLE PROPERTY-BUYING A PROPERTY

Having looked at the costs of acquiring a property, we need now to look at the type of property that you might want to invest in and the areas that you should look in. Obviously, where you choose to buy your property will be your own decision. However, it may be your first time and you may be at a loss as to where to buy, i.e., rural areas or urban areas, the type and cost of property or whether a house or flat. There are several considerations here. The main consideration for a buy-to-let property is the letting potential and security of your asset, i.e., will it appreciate or will it depreciate. As mentioned in the previous chapter, flats are a better investment than houses, as a rule of thumb.

Area

Buying in a built-up area has its advantages and disadvantages. There is usually more demand for property in a built-up area. As far as letting is concerned, there are obvious advantages in that there are normally closer communities, because of the sheer density.

Local services are closer to hand and there is a greater variety of housing for sale.

Transport links are also usually quite good and there are normally plenty of shops. Disadvantages are less space, less privacy, more local activity, noise and pollution, less street parking, more expensive insurance, and different schooling environments to rural environments. There is more detached housing with land, more space and privacy. There is also cleaner air and insurance premiums can be lower. Disadvantages can be isolation, loneliness, lower level of services generally, limited choice of local education, therefore the property will be harder to let.

Choosing your property

You should think carefully when considering purchasing a larger property. You may encounter higher costs prior to letting, and costs that may deter the would-be tenant, which may include:

- Larger more expensive carpeting.
- More furniture. If you are letting your property furnished, then you will need to outlay more at the outset.
- Larger gardens to tend. Although this may have been one of the attractions, large gardens are time consuming, expensive, and hard work.
- Bigger bills.

- More decorating.
- Higher overall maintenance costs.

Purchasing a flat

There are some important points to remember when purchasing a flat. These are common points that are overlooked. For example, if you are buying a flat in a block that is leasehold you will need permission to sublet. This may pose difficulties depending on the freeholder. In addition, the type of cladding on blocks of flats is crucial.

Cladding on blocks

If a person owns a flat of any height with any type of cladding, or none, new safety advice on external walls means that the owners of privately owned flats in England could face months of "cladmin" before being able to sell or remortgage. If you intend to buy a flat, then you should be aware of the cladding issue. Since government advice was extended to blocks of all heights, buyers have been pulling out of sales in low-rise blocks, as well as high-rise. However, buy-to-let investors are excluded from any form of grants or compensation so be very careful here.

*

What fire report do you need?
The government has issued new advice in response to the Grenfell fire in 2017. Building owners must ensure that blocks of any height are safe. Mortgage lenders require a report, for which fire engineers cut holes in buildings to check wall systems. Fewer than 500 engineers have indemnity insurance for this. Cladding and insulation samples are tested to check they match the building's design. If any are combustible the system is deemed safe if a three-storey replica wall passes a fire test. The wait for a test can be eight months to a year. The cost, typically £10,000 to £45,000, is split between all flat owners in the block. The Royal Institution of Chartered Surveyors, the Building Societies Association and UK Finance have launched an external wall system form (EWS1, valid for five years.

What if walls are found unsafe?
The new guidance affects buildings with any flammable cladding or insulation, not only the type that was on Grenfell Tower. Building owners must check that fire breaks are correctly fitted inside walls. In 98 per cent of cases where surveyors have removed cladding to inspect this, they have found defects.

Service charge.
If you purchase a flat in a block, the costs of maintenance of the flat will be your own. However, the costs of maintaining the common

parts will be down to the landlord (usually) paid for by you through a service charge. There has been an awful lot of trouble with service charges, trouble between landlord and leaseholder.

Be very careful if you are considering buying a flat in a block. You should establish levels of service charges and look at accounts.

Try to elicit information from other leaseholders. It could be that there is a leaseholder's organisation, formed to manage their own service charges. This will give you direct control over contracts such as gardening, cleaning, maintenance contracts and cyclical decoration contracts. Better value for money is obtained in this way. In this case, at least you know that the levels will be fair, as no one leaseholder stands to profit. All the above should be considered as the profit that you make from letting your property can be greatly diminished by extra costs such as maintenance charges to a freeholder.

Ground rents

In the light of the recent problems highlighted in Parliament concerning escalating ground rents, rendering properties virtually unsellable, be very careful about the provisions in a lease concerning annual (or other period) ground rent increases. Always take legal advice from a solicitor unconnected to the freeholder. However, there is good news on the horizon for leaseholders, as outlined below.

The Leasehold and Freehold Reform Act 2024

The **Leasehold and Freehold Reform Act 2024** The Act makes it easier and cheaper for leaseholders to buy their freehold, increase standard lease extension terms to 990 years for houses and flats, and provide greater transparency over service charges. The bill will also rebalance the legal costs regime and remove barriers for leaseholders to challenge their landlords' unreasonable charges at Tribunal. The new powers will also help more leaseholders take over the management of their property if they wish to, instead of being stuck with the freeholder's management choice, and we will make this process cheaper for leaseholders. The government will also bring forward further reforms which will extend access to redress schemes and make it easier and cheaper to get the information needed to sell a leasehold home.

Viewing properties

Before you start house hunting, draw up a list of characteristics you will need from a property, such as the number of bedrooms, size of kitchen, garage and study and garden. Take the estate agent's details with you when viewing. Also, take a tape measure with you.

Assess the location of the property. Look at all the aspects and the surroundings. Give some thought as to the impact this will have on the ability to rent. Assess the building. Check the facing aspect of the property, i.e., north, south etc. Check the exterior carefully.

Look for a damp proof course - normally about 15cm from the ground. Look for damp inside and out. Items like leaking rainwater pipes should be noted, as they can be a cause of damp. Look carefully at the windows. Are they rotten? Do they need replacing and so on. Look for any cracks. These should most certainly be investigated. A crack can be symptomatic of something worse, or it can merely be surface. If you are not able to make this judgment, then others should make it for you.

Heating is important. If the house or flat has central heating, you will need to know when it was last tested. Gas central heating should be tested at least once a year. All in all you need to remember that you cannot see everything in a house, particularly on the first visit. A great deal may be being concealed from you. In addition, your own knowledge of property may be slim. A second opinion is a must.

Buying a listed building

Buildings of architectural or historical interest are listed by the Secretary of State for National Heritage following consultation with English Heritage, to protect them against inappropriate alteration.

In Wales, buildings are listed by the Secretary of State for Wales in consultation with CADW (Heritage Wales). In Scotland, they are listed by the Secretary of State for Scotland, in consultation with Historic Scotland. If you intend to carry out work to a listed building, you are likely to need listed building consent for any internal or external work, in addition to planning permission. The conservation officer in the local planning department can provide further information.

Buildings in conservation areas

Local authorities can designate areas of special architectural or historical significance. Conservation areas are protected to ensure that their character or interest is retained. Whole towns or villages may be conservation areas or simply one street.

Strict regulations are laid down for conservation areas. Protection includes all buildings and all types of trees that are larger than 7cm across at 1.5m above the ground. There may be limitations for putting up signs, outbuildings, or items such as satellite dishes. Any developments in the area usually must meet strict criteria, such as the use of traditional or local materials.

This also applies to property in national parks, designated areas of outstanding natural beauty and the Norfolk or Suffolk Broads. Whether or not a property is listed or is deemed to be in a conservation area will show up in a search.

Buying a new house

There are several benefits to buying a new house. You have the advantages of being the first owner. There should not be a demand for too much maintenance or DIY jobs, as the building is new. There will however be a defects period, which usually runs for 6 months for building and 12 months for electrical mechanical. During this period, you should expect minor problems, such as cracking of walls, plumbing etc, which will be the responsibility of the builder.

Energy loss will be minimal. A new house today uses 50 per cent less energy than a house built 15 years ago; consider the savings over an older property. An energy rating indicates how energy efficient a house is.

The National House Building Council uses a rating scheme based on The National Energy Services Scheme, in which houses are given a rating between 0 and 10. A house rated 10 will be very energy efficient and have very low running costs for its size. In addition, an Energy Performance Certificate is mandatory, as described earlier.

Security and safety are built into new houses, smoke alarms are standard and security locks on doors and windows are usually included. When the housing market is slow, developers usually offer incentives to buyers, such as cash back, payment of deposit etc. Always check the freehold transfer concerning charges such as ground rent and service charges.

Building Guarantees

All new houses should be built to certain standards and qualify for one of the building industry guarantees. These building guarantees are normally essential for you to obtain a mortgage and they also make the property attractive to purchasers when you sell. A typical guarantee is the National House Building Council Guarantee (NHBCG).

The process of buying a property

Having considered the costs of the acquisition of a property, the next step is to find the property you want. For the investor, as well as all the considerations listed below, the return on investment will be a key priority.

Looking for a property is a long and sometimes dispiriting process. Trudging around estate agents, sorting through mountains of literature, dealing with estate agents' details, scouring the papers and walking the streets. However, most of us find the property we want at the end of the day. It is then that we can put in our offer. In the times of coronavirus and beyond, estate agents are increasingly reverting to video footage to carry out virtual viewings.

Making an offer

You should put your offer in to the estate agent or direct to the seller, depending on who you are buying from. As discussed earlier, your offer should be based on sound judgment, on what the property is worth and how much rental income after costs that you can derive from it, not on your desire to secure the property at any cost. A survey will help you to arrive at a schedule of works and cost. If you cannot afford to employ a surveyor from a high street firm, then you should try to enlist other help. In addition, you should take a long and careful look at the house yourself, not just a cursory glance. Look at everything and try to get an idea of the likely cost to you of rectifying defects.

However, I cannot stress enough the importance of getting a detailed survey. Eventually, you will be able to make an offer for the property. You should base this offer on sound judgment. You should make it clear that your offer is subject to contract and survey (if you require further examination or wish to carry out a survey after the offer).

Exchange of contracts

Once the buyer and seller are happy with all the details stated in the contract and your conveyancer can confirm that there are no outstanding legal queries, there will be an exchange of contracts.

The sale is now legally binding for both parties. You should arrange the necessary insurance, buildings, and contents from this moment on, as you are now responsible for the property.

Completing a sale

This is the final day of the sale and normally takes place around ten days after the exchange. Exchange and completion can take place on the same day, if necessary, but this is unusual. On the day of completion, you are entitled to vacant possession, and you will receive the keys.

****

CHAPTER 4

Buying a Property at Auction

Although many people will go through the traditional route of acquiring buy-to-let property through an estate agent, there are other routes, one main one being the auction.

Buying at auction requires a different set of skills and you need to know what you are buying, where it is and what the problems are, if any. Why is it being sold at auction? Certainly, you need to act quickly as you need to inspect the property before auction day, arrive at the final bid price that you will not exceed and be prepared to complete within 28 days.

What is a property auction?

The process is very similar to the normal method of private sale. However, for an auction sale the seller and their solicitor carry out all the necessary paperwork and legal investigations prior to the auction. Subject to the property receiving an acceptable bid, the property will be 'sold' on auction day with a legally binding exchange of contracts and a fixed completion date.

Different types of property auction houses

Auction houses vary in size and the amount of business that they conduct and the frequency with which they hold auctions. Most will sell both residential and commercial property and each will have its own style of operation, and fee structure. Large auction houses will hold auctions frequently, perhaps every two months and will have around 250 lots for sale.

A lot of the auctions happen in London but will also be held nearer to home. Most of the large auction houses will deal with property put forward by large institutions, such as banks selling repossessions and local authorities and will advertise the sales in the mainstream media and trade papers. The medium size auction houses will hold auctions as frequently as they can, in regional venues, such as racecourses and conference centers, and depending on stock, usually every two to three months, tending to advertise locally.

The small auction houses will have far fewer lots and will hold their sales in smaller local venues. They may advertise in the local press but more often will trade on word of mouth.

Those who attend auctions

As you might imagine, all sorts of people attend auctions. The common denominator is that they are all interested in buying property.

Property investors are most common at auction, people who are starting out building a portfolio or those who have large portfolios that they wish to expand. They tend to fall into two groups, those who are after capital appreciation, i.e., buy at a low value and build the capital value and those who are looking for rental income. Then there are the property traders who like a quick profit from buying and 'flipping' property. These types usually have intimate knowledge of an area and are well placed to make a quick profit.

Then we have the developers who look for small profitable sites or larger sites where property can be built and sold on. The sites can have existing buildings on them or can be vacant lots with or without planning permission. Last, but not least, we have those people who intend to buy solely for the purpose of owner occupation, look to buy a below- value property that they can redesign and make their own.

What types of property are suitable for auction?
There is strong demand for all types of properties offered at auction. These may be properties requiring updating, those with short leases, development sites with or without planning permission, repossessions, forced sales, investment properties, ground rents, probates, receivership sales and local authority properties. However, any type of property can be sold at auction

and initially the property will be inspected to discuss specific criteria and the current situation.

Extensive research will be carried out by the auction house and advice offered as to whether auction is the appropriate method of sale. The below represents a cross section of what might be found at auction.

Properties for Improvement

Properties in need of updating make ideal auction Lots. They are in great demand from refurbishment specialists and private buyers, keen to undertake a project for their own occupation or for resale. They also appeal to buy-to-let investors who carry out the improvements then retain them as part of a property portfolio.

Tenanted Properties

Residential houses and flats with tenants in residence sell well at auction. Notice doesn't need to be served on tenants, and rental income continues to be received right up to completion.

Residential Investments

Houses in multiple occupation and blocks of flats are sold at auction as valuable investments. Here it is the rent level that determines the sale price, just as much as the building itself.

Development Propositions

Derelict or disused farm buildings, empty commercial premises, buildings with potential for conversion or change of use, can all sell well at auction. In some locations a change to residential can significantly add to the value of a property, in other situations there may be space for additional dwellings or to substantially enlarge the property.

Building Land

There is no better way of ensuring a seller achieves the best price for a building plot or parcel of development land than to offer it for sale by auction. Builders will be able to consult with architects, planners etc., and be ready to bid in the auction room.

Mixed-Use Properties

Properties that have twin uses or a variety of potential future uses are ideal for sale by auction. Retail shops with accommodation above appeal to investors as well as owner-occupiers. Further conversion work can often be undertaken, and the property tailored to suit the purchaser's special requirements.

Commercial Investments-Retail shops, offices, industrial units, garage blocks and parking areas - an ever-increasing number of commercial investments are being sold at auction.

It doesn't matter whether they are vacant or tenanted, with lease renewal soon needed or with a long way to run.

Unique Properties

There are always some rare entries, sought after property and prime locations that need to be sold in a competitive bidding environment. Unexpectedly high prices have been achieved by this route.

Amenity Land and Other Property

Paddocks, meadows, fields, moorings, amenity land and other unusual land parcels are all sold at auction. If it is property or land that is surplus to requirements, the likelihood is a buyer can be found at auction.

Why is property being sold at an auction?

There are several reasons why property is sold at an auction:

- A quick sale is needed, often due to the owner being in financial difficulties or it is a repossession.
- There are structural problems which prevent the property being sold easily in the conventional manner.
- Properties sold by public bodies. Here you get all sort of property, including weird and wonderful properties such as

public toilets and police stations, all of which may have their uses.

- The property is unique and there are no direct comparisons, such as lighthouses and the above-mentioned public toilet.

It is always best to find out why exactly the property is being sold at auction. Is it so difficult to get rid of because of some inherent reason? Ask why is this property at auction and not being sold in the conventional way? Who exactly is the vendor and what if any are the problems stopping it being sold conventionally? The reasons that the property is at auction may be entirely innocent, but it is always worth finding out to avoid future problems.

What happens next?

Once you have found your auction, to receive a complimentary auction catalogue you should contact the auctioneers, and this will give the information about the properties being offered for sale. You can also download a catalogue from the auctioneer's website. The catalogue includes descriptions of the available properties, legal information, viewing arrangements and a guide price, which is purely an indication of a realistic selling price. This should not be taken as a firm asking or selling price and should be relied upon as a guide only. Professional advice must be taken in relation to any lot in which there is an interest.

For lots where viewings are arranged, these are carried out on a block basis and are published in all advertising and in the auction catalogue. Any prospective purchaser is welcome at these viewings and should the scheduled appointments be inconvenient, alternative arrangements can be made.

Any interest must be registered with the Auctioneers in order that prospective purchasers may be kept informed as to the progress of the sale.

Bidding for a property

The lots will be offered, and the bidding taken to the highest possible level and once the gavel falls, the contracts will be exchanged. The buyer purchases the property at the price they bid - this cannot be negotiated, and the stipulated terms cannot be changed. The buyer will then pay 10% of the purchase price on the day and completion occurs 28 days later. The funds are then paid to the seller less the fees of the Auctioneers and those of the seller's solicitor.

The atmosphere of an auction room can be extremely exciting and competitive, and it is often the case that an interested party will bid more than the figure that had previously been set as their maximum. In some cases, the prices achieved at auction can be higher than those achieved by private treaty. The seller will provide a legal pack that may be inspected at any time.

Auctioneers will strongly advise that professional advice is obtained from a legal representative. Details of the seller's solicitors will be available and, should a mortgage be required, it is advisable to have this in place prior to the sale. Again, auctioneers strongly advise that funding is discussed with a professional advisor prior to attending the sale.

The successful buyer will be required to pay 10% of the purchase price on the day, together with a buyer's premium which is normally £250 including VAT. The balance of the purchase price is required on the agreed completion day, and this is normally 28 days after the auction, however this can vary so it is best to check with the auction house.

Finding out legal and survey information

A legal pack is requested from each of the vendor's solicitors and this contains copies of all legal papers, which will be required by any prospective purchasers for them to make an informed decision regarding the purchase of any lot. The pack will include office copy entries and plans, the relevant local authority search, leases (if applicable), Special Conditions of Sale, replies to pre-contract enquiries and any other relevant documents. A copy of these legal packs can usually be obtained from auctioneers for a small charge. Should any additional information be required, the seller's solicitors are listed in the catalogue and can be contacted directly. All legal packs are available for inspection at each auction. Any purchase at auction takes place under the assumption that documentation and the terms of the contract have been read. It is strongly recommended that any potential purchasers carry out full investigations for any lot in which they have an interest, and a survey is an integral part of that investigation.

How is finance arranged?

Should a mortgage be required, approval in principle must be obtained prior to auction. Lenders are now familiar with the auction process and are usually willing to provide a mortgage offer for buyers intending to purchase at auction. A valuation and survey will be required along with legal evidence that there are no issues that will affect the value.

It is essential that the lender can provide funds within the timescale for completion. On the day of the auction, the purchaser will need to pay 10% of the purchase price and must ensure there are cleared funds to pay this amount. Sometimes, finance can be arranged through an Auctioneers on request.

Can lots be bought before auction?

Vendors may consider offers submitted before auction day. Any such offers need to be submitted in writing to an Auctioneers - this will be referred to the vendor and their instruction will be passed on to the prospective purchaser. Any offers will have to be unconditional, and the buyer must be able to exchange contracts and pay the required deposit before auction day. With most auctioneers, no offers are considered within five days of the auction.

What should I take with me to the auction room?
The items required are as follows:
- Deposit cheque or banker's draft for any potential purchase
- Identification - this is legally required under the money laundering regulations. Therefore, a driving licence or passport is required and a current utility bill to show proof of residence.
- Details of solicitors acting on behalf of any potential purchaser.

If a prospective purchaser is unable to attend the auction
If prospective purchasers are unable to attend the sale, it is possible to bid in other ways:
- By telephone - the interested party will be telephoned as the lot is being auctioned.
- By proxy in writing - a member of the auction team will represent the buyer, who has previously specified their maximum bid.

In each case a registration form and cheque to cover the deposit and buyer's fee, are required prior to the date of the auction. A bidder's registration form is printed in the catalogue or alternatively can be obtained from the office.

Will the property be insured when I purchase?
No - the purchaser at auction is responsible for obtaining Building insurance cover from the moment the property is deemed sold to them at auction.

Bidding from your smartphone
A new eBay for homebuyers' is already big business making it easy to bid and buy via smartphone. Homeowners who are wary of the auction room when it comes to buying or selling might prefer a new digital online auction called BidX1 (bidx1.com). It is a bit like online goods market eBay but for property – and the latest sale is today.

Difficulties of raising finance, bargains that turn into bottomless pits, fears about losing deposits, overbidding, and auctioneers plucking "2 bids off the wall" still put many off the traditional "ballroom" auction. But BidX1, up and running in the UK for 18 months, could be modifying that image.

Most significant is the holding of a £4,500 "buyers fee" at registration to enable you to bid. If you win with the highest bid, you must pay a 10 per cent deposit at once and complete the purchase in 20 business days, possibly extended if it is over Christmas. Each time the highest bid is made, the auction automatically extends for a further minute and only closes when there are no further bids. BidX1's registration system for buyers and sellers complies with UK money laundering regulations and enables both sides to see on-screen who is bidding, how much, and when. BidX1's system can also see where the bid is from geographically and on what sort of device it was made.

Customers can view, bid, buy and sell from home on a mobile phone. And it seems the detailed knowledge and visibility of who is bidding and what is of interest to both residential and commercial buyers and sellers is transparent because records can be checked. BidX1's fees are one-and-a- half to two-and-a half per-cent of the sale price, depending on the sale and complexity of what's offered.

****

CHAPTER 5

SOURCING SUITABLE TENANTS AND SUBSEQUENT MANAGEMENT OF YOUR PROPERTY

Whether you are either a landlord or a would - be landlord, you will need to source a tenant for your property. The choice of tenant will be crucial to the success of your business and for your peace of mind.

Letting Agents
An amendment to the Enterprise and Regulatory Reform Act 2013 enabled the Government to require agents to sign up to a redress scheme. The Redress Scheme for Lettings Agency Work and Property Management Work (Requirement to Belong to a Scheme etc) (England) Order 2014 made membership of a scheme a legal requirement with effect from 1 October 2014. The Government also amended the Consumer Rights Act 2015 to require letting agents to publish a full tariff of their fees. (It should be noted that, if you intend to use an agent to manage your properties then ensure that it is signed up to a redress scheme. One such scheme is The

Property Ombudsman Scheme www.tpos.co.uk. The other mandatory scheme is the Property Redress Scheme https://www.theprs.co.uk/consumer/how-it-works. Lettings agents can be fined if they are not signed up to a scheme.

The Tenants Fees Act 2018

The Tenant Fees Act 2018 bans most letting fees and caps tenancy deposits paid by tenants in the private rented sector in England. The ban on tenant fees applies to new or renewed tenancy agreements signed on or after 1 June 2019. From May 2020 it extended to all tenancies. The aim of the Act is to reduce the costs that tenants can face at the outset, and throughout, a tenancy. Tenants will be able to see briefly, what a given property will cost them in the advertised rent with no hidden costs.

The party that contracts the service – the landlord – will be responsible for paying for that service, helping ensure the fees charged reflect the real economic value of the services provided and sharpen letting agents' incentive to compete for landlords' business. Local enforcement authorities have primary responsibility for enforcing this legislation. The Tenant Fees Act created an independent lead enforcement authority to provide advice and information to local authorities on the Act. Bristol city council has been appointed as the lead enforcement authority for lettings.

From 1 June 2019, the only payments that landlords or letting agents can charge to tenants in relation to new contracts are:

- Rent
- a refundable tenancy deposit capped at no more than 5 weeks' rent where the total annual rent is less than £50,000, or 6 weeks' rent where the total annual rent is £50,000 or above
- a refundable holding deposit (to reserve a property) capped at no more than 1 week's rent
- payments associated with early termination of the tenancy, when requested by the tenant
- payments capped at £50 (or reasonably incurred costs, if higher) for the variation, assignment, or novation of a tenancy
- payments in respect of utilities, communication services, TV license and Council Tax
- a default fee for late payment of rent and replacement of a lost key/security device giving access to the housing, where required under a tenancy agreement.

Online lettings agents

The rise of online letting agents has been rapid and they now account for a growing percentage of the market. The attractions are obvious, the costs. One of the biggest online property agents,

Sourcing Suitable Tenants and Management of Your Property

EasyProperty.com offers 'pick and mix' services ranging from £10 a week for adverts on Right Move, Prime Location and Zoopla to 3% commission for full property management. For a tenant finding service with all the frills, such as hosted viewings and professional photos to check-in the total bill would be £445. This equates to less than half the commission charged by high-street agents. However, there can be drawbacks. The main drawback is accessibility. If you have your contract with a local agent, they will be there when you want them. Online tends to be one step removed. You are strongly advised to consider what it is you want before entering any deal with an online agent. If you do appoint an agent to manage a property you should agree at the outset, in writing, exactly what constitutes management.

Failure to understand the deal can cost you dearly. For example, in a lot of cases, an agent will charge you a fixed fee for finding a tenant but will then exercise the right that they have given themselves in the initial contract to sign a new agreement and charge another month's rent after the tenancy has expired. In this way they will charge you a months rent every six months for doing nothing at all.

Managing properties online

A free new letting platform enables buy-to-let landlords to manage their properties with the same tools as larger investors.

Planetrent.co.uk takes you through every step of finding tenants, managing repairs, and ensuring legal compliance. The company behind the platform is Ringley Group, which manages 12,000 homes for corporate investors.

The platform's launch was brought forward by two months to help people to cope with social distancing. Pay-as-you-go extras include advertising on Rightmove and Zoopla (£60), digital contract signing (£20) and reference checks (£20). However, check these prices as they may change.

What agents do

Agents will typically look after the following:
- Check tenants have the 'Right to Rent' Landlords must ensure tenants can legally reside in the UK before letting to them.

The penalty for renting to someone without the right to rent is a fine or even imprisonment. It should be noted that a substantial increase in the penalties has come into effect from the start of 2024. The penalties are as follows:

Per occupier (rented accommodation) first breach £10,000 repeat breach £20,000. Per lodger (private household) first breach £5,000 repeat breach £10,000. These rules are applicable from 2024.

- Give tenants a copy of the 'How to Rent' guide This guide lists landlord obligations and tenants' rights. You must either give tenants a hard copy or email it to them as an attachment. A link to the guide is not enough. Landlords who fail to do this are unable to evict tenants under a Section 21 Notice (Or 6A as appropriate).
- Transfer the utility bills and the council tax into the name of the tenant.
- Sign agreements and take up references.
- Paying for repairs, although an agent will only normally do this if rent is being paid directly to them and they can make appropriate deductions.
- Chase rent arrears.
- Serve notices of intent to seek possession if the landlord instructs them to do so. An agent cannot commence court proceedings except through a solicitor.
- Visit the property at regular intervals and check that the tenants are not causing any damage.
- Deal with neighbor complaints.
- Banking rental receipts if the landlord is abroad
- Dealing with housing benefit departments if necessary. The extent to which agents do any or all the above really depends on the caliber of the agent. It also depends on the type of agreement you have with the agent. Like your initial

business plan, you should be very clear about what it is you want from the agent and how much they charge.

All buy-to-let landlords should consider taking out insurance for non-payment of rent. *Beware! There are many so-called rental agencies, which have sprung up since the advent of "Buy to Let". These agents are not professional, do not know a thing about property management, are shady and should be avoided like the plague.*

Shop around and seek a reputable agent. A typical management fee might be 10-15 percent of the rent, although there is lots of competition and lower prices can be obtained.

As stated, there are many ways of charging, and you should be clear about this.

It is illegal for agencies to charge tenants for giving out a landlord's name and address. Most agencies will charge the landlord.

Advertisements

If you decide to dispense with the use of an agent, the classified advertisement section of local papers is a good place to seek potential tenants. Local papers are obviously cheaper than the national papers such as the Evening Standard in London or the broadsheets such as the Guardian. The type of newspaper you advertise in will largely reflect what type of customer you are looking for. An advert in the pages of the Times would indicate that you are looking for a well-heeled professional and this would be reflected in the type of property that you have to let.

There are many free ad papers, and you may want to go to student halls of residence or hospitals to attract a potential tenant.

When you do advertise, you should clearly indicate the type of property, in what area, what is required, i.e., male or female only, and the rent. You should try and avoid abbreviations as this causes confusion.

The public sector

One other source of income is the local authority or housing association. Quite often, your property will be taken out of your hands under a five-year contract and you will receive a rental income paid direct for this period, with agreed increases. However, the local authority or housing association will demand a high standard before taking the property off your hands. Quite often the rent achieved will be lower than a comparable market rent, in return for full management and secure income.

If you wish to try this avenue, then you should contact your local authority or nearest large association.

Company lets

Where the tenant is a company rather than an individual, the tenancy agreement will be like an assured shorthold but will not be bound by the six-month rule (see further on for details of assured shorthold tenancies). Company lets can be from any length of time, from a week to several years, or as long you like. The major difference between contracts and standard assured shorthold agreements is that the contract will be tailored to individual needs, and the agreement is bound by the provisions of contract law. Company tenancies are bound by the provisions of contract law and not by the Housing Acts. Note: if you are considering letting to a company you must use a letting agent or solicitor. Most companies will insist on it. The advantages of a landlord letting to a company are:

- A company or embassy has no security of tenure and therefore cannot be a sitting tenant.
- A company cannot seek to reduce the rent by statutory interventions.
- Rental payments are often made quarterly or six months in advance.
- The financial status of a company is usually more secure than that of an individual.

- Company tenants often require long-term lets to accommodate staff relocating on contracts of between one and five years.
- *The main disadvantage of company lets are:*
- A company tenancy can only be to a bona fide company or embassy, not to a private individual.
- A tenancy to a partnership would not count as a company let and may have some security of tenure.
- If the tenant is a foreign government, the diplomatic status of the occupant must be ascertained, as the courts cannot enforce breaches of contract with somebody who possesses diplomatic immunity.
- A tenancy to a foreign company not registered in the UK may prove time consuming and costly if it becomes necessary to pursue claims for unpaid rent or damage through foreign courts.

Short lets

Although company lets can be of any length, it is becoming increasingly popular for companies to rent flats from private landlords on short lets. A short let is any let of less than six months. But here, it is essential to check the rules with any borough concerned. Some boroughs will not allow lets for less than three months, as they do not want to encourage transient people in the neighborhood.

Short lets are only applicable in large cities where there is a substantial shifting population. Business executives on temporary relocation, actors and others involved in television production or film work, contract workers and visiting academics are examples of people who might require a short let. From a landlord's point of view, short lets are an excellent idea if you must vacate your own home for seven or eight months, say, and do not want to leave it empty.

Short-let tenants provide useful extra income as well as keeping an eye on the place. Or if you are buying a new property and have not yet sold the old one, it can make good business sense to let it to a short-let tenant. Short-let tenants are, usually, from a landlord's point of view, excellent blue-chip occupants. They are busy professionals, high earners, out all day and used to high standards. As the rent is paid by the company there is no worry for the landlord on this score either.

A major plus of short lets is that they command between 20-50 percent more rent than the optimum market rent for that type of property. The one downside of short lets is that no agency can guarantee permanent occupancy.

Student lets
Students usually come in groups and don't have many belongings, so they want houses or flats with lots of furnished bedrooms and

large communal spaces. More than one toilet or bathroom would be a bonus that can help you charge higher rents.

Advantages of letting to students:
- Typically, students are not overly fussy about having state-of-the-art accommodation. For many it might be their first rental and they're more interested in being with their friends. Older properties with multiple rooms are ideal.
- You can charge rent per room. Since there are often more tenants in a student let than there would be family members in a similar property, especially if you have converted a living area into another bedroom, you can expect high returns.
- It is relatively easy to find tenants, particularly if you are close to a university campus!
- Students move on, so you are not tied into any long-term contracts.
- Generally, students are reliable tenants, easy-going and undemanding. And best of all there's a new pool of them searching for accommodation every year.

Disadvantages of student lettings
- Demand for privately let student housing is being affected by the rise of purpose-built private student accommodation. Research your area thoroughly.

- Bills for maintenance and repairs will probably be higher than usual but then you can offset this against the cost of not needing to provide expensive furniture and décor.
- You should always have a guarantor as students are coming from their family home.
- You may have a few months where your property is vacant during the summer holidays until the new term starts, but many student landlords insist on 12-month leases.
- You might have to deal with noise complaints from neighbors or the local council if your tenants like to party.

While you are weighing up the advantages and disadvantages to student lettings, consider whether you will need to have certain accreditations as well. A property that is let to three or more tenants who are not related could be classed as a House in Multiple Occupation (HMO), in which case you will need to be licensed by your local authority. You can also become an accredited landlord by a university, which means that you will be a recommended and trusted first port of call for students seeking new digs. Imagine how easy it would be to find tenants that way!

The DSS and housing benefit

Very few letting agencies or landlords will touch DSS or housing benefit tenants. However, as with student lets, there is another side of the coin. Quite often it is essential for a tenant on HB to have a guarantor, usually a homeowner, before signing a tenancy. Then it is up to the machinations of the benefit system to ensure that the landlord receives rent. The rent is assessed by a benefit officer, with the rent usually estimated at market price. There are rent levels set for each area that the benefit officer will not go above. A deposit is paid normally, and rent can be paid direct to the landlord. This will require the tenant's consent No other conditions should be accepted by a private landlord. Rent certainly should not be paid direct to the tenant. Although tenants on HB have a bad name, due to stereotyping, there are many reasons why a person may be on benefit and if housing benefit tenancies are managed well.

Holiday lets

Before the Housing Act 1988 became law, many landlords advertised their properties as holiday lets to bypass the then rules regarding security of tenure. Strictly speaking, a holiday let is a property let for no more than a month to any one tenant. If the same tenant renews for another month, then the landlord is breaking the law.

Nowadays, holiday lets must be just that; let for a genuine holiday. If you have a flat or cottage that you wish to let for holiday purposes, whether you live in it yourself for part of the year, you are entering into a quite different agreement with the tenant.

Holiday lets are not covered by the Housing Act. The contract is finalised by exchange of letters with the tenant where they place a deposit, and the owner confirms the booking. If the let is not for a genuine holiday, you may have problems in evicting the tenant.

Certain services must be provided for the let to be deemed a holiday let. Cleaning services and changes of bed linen are essential. The amount paid by the holidaymaker will usually include utilities but would exclude use of the telephone, fax machine etc.

If you have a property that you think is suitable for a holiday let or wish to invest in one, there are numerous companies who will put you on to their books. However, standards are high and there are a certain number of criteria to be met, such as safety checks, before they consider taking you on. If possible, you should talk to someone with some experience of this type of let before entering into an agreement with an agency.

The usual problems may arise, such as ensuring occupancy all year round and the maintenance of your property, which will be higher due to a high turnover. In addition to the above, the tax situation is changing for those with holiday lets which will mean the loss of certain allowances and the tightening up of others.

This is discussed further in chapter 13, which deals with taxation issues.

Sourcing Suitable Tenants and Management of Your Property

Holiday lets-Letting through Airbnb or similar sites

Over the last few years, landlords have increasingly turned to companies like Airbnb to let their properties. However, what started out as a good concept has, as usual, been undermined by those looking for a quick return.

A growing number of property owners are earning extra income by using short term let Companies such as Airsorted and GuestReady have popped up in the past few years and have reported phenomenal demand. They list customers' properties on sites such as Booking.com, Airbnb and HomeAway and manage the booking process from start to finish.

These short-term lettings agencies off a management service, which, for a fee, handle every aspect of each booking which also includes (if you pay for it) the changing of towels and sheets and just about everything to make sure that the property is ready for each short-term guest. The management companies tend to operate in urban areas and typically levy a percentage fee. **Pass the Keys** starts at 12% of rental income plus VAT. It operates in cities including Brighton, Bristol, and Glasgow.

Guest ready charges 12%. for a basic service or 20% for premium which includes insurance professional photography for the listing and 24/7 guest support. It operates in cities such as London. Edinburgh and Manchester.

Airsorted covers locations including Bath, Dublin, Cambridge, and London.

Even when fees are considered, customers can earn more by using a service. However, if you are considering offering a short-term let check your mortgage. Properties specifically aimed at holiday letting will require a special mortgage. Most buy to let lenders will not allow holiday lets, usually requiring tenancies of at least six months.

Lenders offering holiday-let mortgages include Leeds, Market Harborough and Furness Building Societies. However, these mortgages typically preclude properties on a holiday site, as the lender will typically want to sell on the open market.

As short lets are classified as holiday lets, the owners of such lets can deduct interest payments from the rent before calculating their tax liability providing they can satisfy certain tests. This includes letting their property for at least 105 days a year.

Holiday-let owners can also claim the full cost of furnishing the property. For regular buy-to-let, it is repairs only.

When showing the property to the tenant-For traditional lettings, once you have found a tenant, the next stage is to decide a time for viewing the property.

It is a good idea to make all appointments on the same day to avoid wasting time. If you decide on a likely tenant, it is wise to take up references yourself if you are not using an agency who will do this for you. This will normally be a previous landlord's reference and a bank reference plus a personal reference. Only when these have been received and you have established that the person(s) is/are safe should you go ahead. Make sure that no keys have been handed over until the cheque has been cleared and you are in receipt of a month's rent and a month's deposit.

Deposits-Tenancy Deposit Protection Scheme

The Tenancy Deposit Protection Scheme was introduced to protect all deposits paid to landlords after 6th April 2007. After this date, landlords and/or agents must use a government authorised scheme to protect deposits. The need for such a scheme has arisen because of the historical problem with deposits.

From 1 June 2019, the maximum tenancy deposit is equal to 5 weeks' rent. This limit applies to deposits taken from all assured shorthold tenants, lodgers, and students in halls of residence if the yearly rent is less than £50,000. The scheme works as follows:

Moving into a property

At the beginning of a new tenancy agreement, the tenant will pay a deposit to the landlord or agent as usual. Within 30 days the landlord is required to give the tenant details of how the deposit is going to be protected including:

- the address of the rented property

- how much deposit you've paid
- how the deposit is protected
- the name and contact details of the tenancy deposit protection (TDP) scheme and its dispute resolution service
- their (or the letting agency's) name and contact details
- the name and contact details of any third party that's paid the deposit
- why they would keep some or all the deposit
- how to apply to get the deposit back
- what to do if you can't get hold of the landlord at the end of the tenancy
- what to do if there's a dispute over the deposit.

There are three tenancy deposit schemes that a landlord can opt for:

My Deposits

www.mydeposits.co.uk

info.custodial@mydeposits.co.uk

The Tenancy Deposit Scheme

www.tds.gb.com

The Deposit Protection Service

www.depositprotection.com

contactus@depositprotection.com

The schemes above fall into two categories, insurance-based schemes, and custodial schemes.

Custodial Scheme
- The tenant pays the deposit to the landlord
- The landlord pays the deposit into the scheme
- Within 14 days of receiving the deposit, the landlord must give the tenant prescribed information
- A the end of the tenancy, if the landlord and tenant have agreed how much of the deposit is to be returned, they will tell the scheme which returns the deposit, divided in the way agreed by the parties.
- If there is a dispute, the scheme will hold the disputed amount until the dispute resolution service or courts decide what is fair
- The interest accrued by deposits in the scheme will be used to pay for the running of the scheme and any surplus will be used to offer interest to the tenant, or landlord if the tenant isn't entitled to it.

Insurance based schemes
- The tenant pays the deposit to the landlord
- The landlord retains the deposit and pays a premium to the insurer (this is the key difference between the two schemes)

Within 14 days of receiving a deposit the landlord must give the tenant prescribed information.
- At the end of the tenancy if the landlord and tenant agree how the deposit is to be divided or otherwise then the landlord will return the amount agreed
- If there is a dispute, the landlord must hand over the disputed amount to the scheme for safekeeping until the dispute is resolved. If for any reason the landlord fails to comply, the insurance arrangements will ensure the return of the deposit to the tenant if they are entitled to it.
- If a landlord or agent hasn't protected a deposit with one of the above, then the tenant can apply to the local county court for an order for the landlord either to protect the deposit or repay it.

Rental guarantees

The landlord is always advised to obtain a guarantor if there is any potential uncertainty as to payment of rent. One example is where the tenant is on benefits. The guarantor will be expected to assume responsibility for the rent if the tenant ceases to pay at any time during the term of the tenancy.

****

CHAPTER 6

WHAT SHOULD BE PROVIDED UNDER THE TENANCY?

When you let a property, you have the choice of letting it furnished or unfurnished. There is a market for both, but most properties will at least have white goods installed.

Furniture

A landlord's decision whether to furnish property will depend on the sort of tenant that he is aiming to find. The actual legal distinction between furnished property and unfurnished property has faded into insignificance.

If a landlord does let a property as furnished, then the following would be the absolute minimum:
- Seating, such as a sofa and an armchair.
- Cabinet or sideboard.
- Kitchen tables and chairs.
- Cooker and refrigerator.
- Bedroom furniture.

- Even unfurnished lets, however, are expected to come complete with a basic standard of furniture, particularly carpets and kitchen goods.

If the landlord does supply electrical equipment, then he or she will be responsible for carrying out annual checks along with annual checks on the boiler.

Services in flatted properties

Service charges, and the paying of these charges, will be the responsibility of the leaseholder. They will be included in the rent charged by the leaseholder to the tenant of the flat. However, the leaseholder should have some idea of the law in this area as it will be a cost which needs to be considered.

Usually, a landlord (freeholder) will only provide services to a tenant if the property is a flat situated in a block or house split into flats or is a house on a private estate. The services will include cyclical painting and maintenance, usually on a three-to-four-year basis (flats) and gardening and cleaning plus repairs to the communal areas, plus communal electricity bills and water rates. These services should be outlined in the agreement and administered within a strict framework of law. The 1985 Landlord and Tenant Act Section 18-30 as amended by the 1987 LTA and the

What Should Be Provided Under the Tenancy

1996 Housing Act as amended by the 2002 Commonhold and Leasehold Reform Act are the main areas of law.

The landlord has rigid duties imposed within the Acts, such as the need to gain estimates before commencing works and to consult with residents where the cost exceeds £250 per flat. The landlord must give the tenant 28 days notice of works to be carried out and a further 28 days to consider estimates, inviting feedback.

Tenants (leaseholders) have the right to see audited accounts and invoices relating to work. Service charges, as an extra payment over and above the rent are always contentious and it is an area that landlords need to be aware of if they are to manage professionally.

Insurance

Strictly speaking, there is no legal duty on either landlord or tenant to insure the property. However, it is highly advisable for the landlord to provide buildings insurance as he/she stands to lose a lot more in the event of a disaster than the tenant. In addition, mortgagors will always want insurance in place to protect their own investment. A landlord letting property for a first time would be well advised to consult his/her insurance company before letting as there are different criteria to observe when a property is let and not to inform the company could invalidate the policy.

At the end of the tenancy

The tenancy agreement will normally spell out the obligations of the tenant at the end of the term. Essentially, the tenant will have an obligation to:

- Have kept the interior clean and tidy and in a good state of repair and decoration.
- Have not caused any damage.
- Have replaced anything that they have broken.
- Replace or pay for the repair of anything that they have damaged.
- Pay for the laundering of the linen.
- Pay for any other laundering and put anything that they have moved or removed back to how it was.

Sometimes a tenancy agreement will include for the tenants paying for anything that is soiled at their own expense, although sensible wear and tear is allowed for. The landlord will normally be able to recover any loss from the deposit that the tenant has given on entering the premises (see previous chapter for details of the Deposit Protection Schemes). However, sometimes, the tenants will withhold rent for the last month to recoup their deposit. The introduction of the Deposit Protection Schemes has made this more difficult in practice. It is up to the landlord to negotiate reimbursement for any damage caused, but this should be within reason. There is a remedy, which can be pursued in the small claims court if the tenants refuse to pay but this is rarely successful.

****

CHAPTER 7

KNOWING THE LAW

Explaining the law

As a landlord, or potential landlord, it is very important to understand the rights and obligations of yourself and your tenant, exactly what can and what cannot be done once the tenancy agreement has been signed and the tenant has moved into the property. To fully understand the law, we should begin by looking at the main types of relationship between people and their homes.

The freehold and the lease

In law, there are two main types of ownership and occupation of property. These are: freehold and leasehold. These arrangements are very old indeed.

Freehold

If a person owns their property outright (usually with a mortgage) then they are a freeholder. The only claims to ownership over and above their own might be those of the building society or the bank, which lent them the money to buy the property.

They will re-possess the property if the mortgage payments are not kept up with. In certain situations, though, the local authority (council) for an area can affect a person's right to do what they please with their home even if they are a freeholder. This will occur when planning powers are exercised, for example, to prevent the carrying out of alterations without consent. The local authority for your area has many powers and we will be referring to these regularly.

Leasehold
If a person lives in a property owned by someone else and has a written agreement allowing them to occupy the flat or house for a period i.e., giving them permission to live in that property, then they will, in the main, have a lease and either be a leaseholder or a tenant of a landlord. The main principle of a lease is that a person has been given permission by someone else to live in his or her property for a period. The person giving permission could be either the freeholder or another leaseholder. The tenancy agreement is one type of lease.

The position of the tenant
The tenant will usually have an agreement for a shorter period than the typical leaseholder. Whereas the leaseholder will, for example,

have an agreement for ninety-nine years, the tenant will have an agreement.

This will run either from week to week or month to month (periodic tenancy) or is for a fixed term, for example, six months or one-year. These arrangements are the most common types of agreement between the private landlord and tenant. The agreement itself will state whether it is a fixed term or periodic tenancy. If an agreement has not been issued it will be assumed to be a fixed-term tenancy.

Both periodic and fixed term tenants will usually pay a sum of rent regularly to a landlord in return for permission to live in the property (more about rent and service charges later)

The tenancy agreement

The tenancy agreement is the usual arrangement under which one person will live in a property owned by another. Before a tenant moves into a property, he/she will have to sign a tenancy agreement drawn up by a landlord or landlord's agent. A tenancy agreement is a contract between landlord and tenant. It is important to realize that when you sign a tenancy agreement, you have signed a contract with another person, which governs the way in which they will live in your property.

The protected tenancy - the meaning of the term

As a basic guide, if a person is a private tenant and signed their current agreement with a landlord before 15th January 1989 then they will, in most cases, be a protected tenant with all the rights relating to protection of tenure.

These are considerable and protection is provided under the 1977 Rent Act. In practice, there are not many protected tenancies left and the tenant will usually be signing an assured shorthold tenancy.

The assured shorthold tenancy - what it means

If the tenant entered into an agreement with a landlord after 15th January 1989, then they will, in most cases, be an assured tenant. We will discuss assured tenancies in more depth in chapter three.

In brief, there are various types of assured tenancy. The assured shorthold is usually a fixed term version of the assured tenancy and enables the landlord to recover their property after six months and to vary the rent after this time. *It is this tenancy that a private tenant will be signing.*

Other types of agreement

In addition to the above tenancy agreements, there are other types of agreement sometimes used in privately rented property. One of these is the company let, as we discussed in the last chapter, and another is the license agreement. The person signing such an agreement is called a licensee.

Licenses will only apply in special circumstances where the licensee cannot be given sole occupation of his home and therefore can only stay for a short period with minimum rights.

What is inserted in the agreement?

Typically, any tenancy agreement will show:

- The name and address of the landlord and will state the names of the tenant(s). The type of tenancy agreement that is signed should be clearly indicated. In the main, in the private sector, the agreement between landlord and tenant will be an assured shorthold tenancy.
- Date of commencement of tenancy and rent payable. The date the tenancy began and the duration (fixed term or periodic) plus the amount of rent payable should be clearly shown, along with who is responsible for any other charges, such as water rates, council tax etc, and a description of the property you are renting out.
- In addition to the rent that must be paid there should be a clear indication of when a rent increase can be expected. This information is sometimes shown in other conditions of tenancy, which should be given to the tenant when they

move into their home. The conditions of tenancy will set out landlords and tenants rights and obligations.
- Services provided under the tenancy and service of notice. If services are provided, i.e., if a service charge is payable, this should be indicated in the agreement. The tenancy agreement should clearly indicate the address to which notices on the landlord can be served by the tenant.
- for example, because of repair problems or notice of leaving the property. The landlord has a legal requirement to indicate this.
- Tenants' obligations. The tenancy agreement will either be a basic document with the above information or will be more comprehensive. Either way, there will be a section beginning "the tenant agrees." Here the tenant will agree to move into the property, pay rent, use the property as an only home, not cause a nuisance to others, take responsibility for certain internal repairs, not sublet the property, i.e., create another tenancy, and various other things depending on the property.
- Landlords' obligations. There should also be another section "the landlord agrees".
- Here, the landlord is contracting with the tenant to allow quiet enjoyment of the property. The landlord's repairing responsibilities are also usually outlined.

- Ending a tenancy. Finally, there should be a section entitled "ending the tenancy". This will outline the ways in which landlord and tenant can end the agreement. The landlord can only end a fixed term assured shorthold tenancy by issuing a s21 notice. (so called because it arises out of section 21 of the Housing Act 1988, as amended) two months prior to the end of the tenancy.
- Many landlords issued this notice at the outset of the tenancy. However, the Deregulation Act 2015 has effectively stopped this practice and states that the landlord cannot now service the notice until the tenant has been in occupation for at least four months. The tenant, after the expiry of the fixed term, can give one month's notice to leave. One more point worth noting is that, if the landlord issues notice, in the required format, by text or email this is likely to be accepted as valid notice.

The landlord must serve a notice by using Form 6A (replacing s21) for all tenancies created on or after October 1st, 2015. This form must be used for all ASTs created on or after 1 October 2015 except for statutory periodic tenancies which have come into being on or after 1 October 2015 at the end of fixed term ASTs created before 1 October 2015.

It is also in this section of the tenancy that the landlord should refer to the "grounds for possession". Grounds for possession are circumstances where the landlord will apply to court for possession of his/her property.

Some of these grounds relate to what is in the tenancy, i.e., the responsibility to pay rent and to not cause a nuisance. Other grounds do not relate to the contents of the tenancy directly, but more to the law governing that tenancy. The grounds for possession are very important, as they are used in any court case brought against the tenant. Unfortunately, they are not always indicated in the tenancy agreement. The sample tenancy agreement in the appendix contains grounds for possession.

The responsibility of the landlord to provide a rent book

If the tenant is a weekly periodic tenant, the landlord must provide him/her with a rent book and commits a criminal offence if he/she does not do so. This is outlined in the Landlord and Tenant Act 1985 sections 4 - 7. Under this Act any tenant can ask in writing the name and address of the landlord. The landlord must reply within twenty-one days of asking. As most tenancies nowadays are fixed term assured shortholds then it is not strictly necessary to provide a tenant with a rent book. *However, for the purposes of efficiency, and your own records, it is always useful to have a rent book and sign it each time rent is collected, or a standing order is paid.*

Overcrowding

It is important to understand, when signing a tenancy agreement, that it is not permitted to allow the premises to become overcrowded, i.e., to allow more people than was originally intended, (which is outlined in the agreement) to live in the property. If a tenant does, then the landlord can take action to evict.

****

CHAPTER 8

UNDERSTANDING RENT AND THE SOURCES OF RENT

As should have become apparent by now, rent is the key to your survival as a residential landlord and it is vital to understand the issues surrounding rent and the payment of rent, in particular the various sources of rent, including housing benefit. In the last few years, with the effects of the coronavirus on people's ability to pay rent, and the difficulty of evicting a tenant during the pandemic, (although in 2024, this has now passed, and more tenants are being given no fault eviction notices) attention to how and where rent comes from is very important.

Rent increases for assured shorthold tenants

The amount of rent a tenant must pay is set out in the tenancy agreement or agreed verbally with the tenant. Rent increases must follow certain rules. Landlords can charge a market rent for an assured shorthold tenancy.

Agreeing to pay a new rent

A landlord can increase the rent if the tenant agrees. It usually counts as agreeing to a new rent if the tenant pays a rent increase, even if they are unhappy about it.

Signing a new contract

If a tenant signs a new tenancy agreement, they must pay the rent amount set out in the new agreement.

During a fixed-term tenancy

A landlord can't increase the rent during a fixed-term tenancy unless there is a rent review clause in the agreement that says the rent can be increased. Most assured shorthold tenancies start with a fixed term.

Rent increases when a rent review clause is used

A landlord can use a rent review clause in the tenancy agreement to increase the rent if the contract contains one. A rent review clause usually sets out when the increase will happen and how much notice the tenant will get and how the rent can be increased (for example, a formula for calculating the new amount).

Any rent review clause won't apply after the tenancy's fixed term ends unless the tenancy continues as a contractual periodic tenancy. This happens if the tenancy agreement says something

Understanding Rent and the Sources of rent

like: contract is for a term of 12 months and thereafter from month to month'.

Rent increases using a section 13 notice

Section 13 (2) of the Housing Act 1988 provides for a landlord to increase rent in an assured shorthold tenancy agreement by issuing a Section 13 Notice.

If the rent is not stated in the tenancy agreement and the tenant does not agree to the proposed rent increase. (Or if the rent review clause no longer applies). Your landlord must use Form 4 to give you valid notice. (See appendix). The section 13 procedure can only be used to increase the rent once a year. The tenant must get at least 1 month's notice of the increase if they have a weekly or monthly tenancy. They are entitled to more notice if the tenancy period is longer than a month. The landlord can serve the notice during the fixed term of the tenancy, but the rent increase can't take effect until after the fixed term has ended.

If the tenancy didn't start with a fixed term, a section 13 notice can't be used during the first year. If the tenant doesn't challenge the increase, the new rent applies after the notice expires.

Right to challenge a proposed section 13 increase

A tenant can apply to a tribunal for rent disputes to challenge a proposed section 13 rent increase. The tribunal must receive their application before the rent increase date given on the notice. They must continue to pay rent at the previously agreed rate until the tribunal makes its decision. The tribunal can decide that the tenant has accepted the rent increase if they pay it.

If the tribunal decides to increase the rent, the new rent usually applies from the rent increase date on the section 13 notice.

Negotiating the amount of an increase

It costs landlords time and money to re-let a property, so the tenant can try negotiating with the landlord if they:

- don't want to accept the rent increase at all
- would accept a lower rent increase
- want the increase to be rolled out in stages over a period.

Private tenants Local Housing Allowance

If your tenants cannot work for some reason, then they will be entitled to Local Housing Allowance (LHA). Their eligible rent amount is either their Local Housing Allowance (LHA) rate or their actual rent, whichever is lower. It is important to note that LHA has remained static for a number of years whilst rents have increased. It has been proposed that an increase is made to ensure that tenants can avoid accumulating arrears and possible eviction. The LHA rate is based on: where they live and their household size.

Understanding Rent and the Sources of rent

How much they can get

How much they get depends on:

- the lower figure of their 'eligible' rent or LHA rate
- their household income including benefits, pensions, and savings (over £6,000)
- their circumstances (for example your age or whether you have a disability)
- change address
- have a break in your claim for Housing Benefit

How the tenant is paid

For a private tenant it's paid into their bank or building society account (rarely by cheque)

Council tax and the tenant

Council tax is based on properties, or dwellings, and not individual people. This means that there is one bill for each individual dwelling, rather than separate bills for each person. The number and type of people who live in the dwelling may affect the size of the final bill. A discount of 25 percent is given for people who live alone. Each property is placed in a valuation band with different properties paying depending on their individual value.

Tenants who feel that their home has been placed in the wrong valuation band can appeal to their local authority council tax department.

Who must pay the council tax?
In most cases the tenant occupying the dwelling will have to pay the council tax. That person is known as the 'liable person'. Nobody under the age of 18 can be a liable person. Couples living together will both be liable even if there is only one name appearing on the bill. However, a landlord will be responsible for paying the council tax where:

- there are several households living in one dwelling where households pay rent separately or:
- where people are under the age of 18.
- the people who live in the property are all asylum seekers who are not entitled to claim benefits including council tax benefits.
- the people who are staying in the property are there temporarily and have their main homes elsewhere; or
- the property is a care home, hospital, hostel, or women's refuge.

Although the landlord has the responsibility for paying the council tax, he or she will normally try to pass on the increased cost through rents. However, there is a set procedure for a landlord to follow if he/she wishes to increase rent. The rules covering council tax liability can be obtained from a Citizens Advice Bureau or from your local authority council tax department.

****

CHAPTER 9

CARRYING OUT REPAIRS AND IMPROVEMENTS TO A PROPERTY

Repairs and improvements generally: The landlord and tenants' obligations

Repairs are essential works to keep the property in good order. Improvements and alterations to the property, e.g., the installation of a shower, will enhance the property.

As we have seen, most tenancies are periodic, i.e., week-to-week or month-to-month. If a tenancy falls into this category or is a fixed-term tenancy for less than seven years, and began after October 1961, then a landlord is legally responsible for most major repairs to the flat or house. If a tenancy began after 15th January 1989, then, in addition to the above responsibility, the landlord is also responsible for repairs to common parts and service fittings.

The area of law dealing with the landlord and tenants repairing obligations is the 1985 Landlord and Tenant Act, section 11. This section of the Act is known as a covenant and cannot be excluded by informal agreement between landlord and tenant. In other words, the landlord is legally responsible whether he or she likes it or not. Parties to a tenancy, however, may make an application to a court mutually to vary or exclude this section.

Example of repairs a landlord is responsible for:
- Leaking roofs and guttering.
- Rotting windows.
- Rising damp.
- Damp walls.
- Faulty electrical wiring.
- Dangerous ceilings and staircases.
- Faulty gas and water pipes.
- Broken water heaters and boilers.
- Broken lavatories, sinks or baths.

In shared housing the landlord must see that shared halls, stairways, kitchens, and bathrooms are maintained and kept clean and lit. Normally, tenants are responsible only for minor repairs, e.g., broken door handles, cupboard doors, etc. Tenants will also be responsible for decorations unless they have been damaged because of the landlord's failure to do repairs. A landlord will be responsible for repairs only if the repair has been reported. It is therefore important to keep a record of repairs in writing. If the repair is not carried out, then action can be taken.

Carrying Out Repairs and Improvements to a Property

Damages can also be claimed along with compensation, with the appropriate amount being the reduction in the value of the premises to the tenant caused by the landlord's failure to repair. If the tenant carries out the repairs, then the amount expended will represent the decrease in value. The tenant does not have the right to withhold rent because of a breach of repairing covenant by the landlord. However, depending on the repair, the landlord will not have a very strong case in court if rent is withheld.

Reporting repairs to landlords

The tenant must tell the landlord or the person collecting the rent straight away when a repair needs doing. It is advisable that it is in writing, listing the repairs that need to be done. Once a tenant has reported a repair the landlord must do it within a reasonable period. What is reasonable will depend on the nature of the repair.

The tenants' rights whilst repairs are being carried out

The landlord must ensure that the repairs are done in an orderly and efficient way with minimum inconvenience to the tenant. If the works are disruptive or if property or decorations are damaged the tenant can apply to the court for compensation or, if necessary, for an order to make the landlord behave reasonably. If the landlord genuinely needs the house empty to do the work, he/she can ask the tenant to vacate it and can, if necessary, get a court order against the tenant.

A written agreement should be drawn up making it clear that the tenant can move back in when the repairs are completed and stating what the arrangements for fuel charges and rent are.

Can the landlord put the rent up after doing repairs?

If there is a service charge for maintenance, the landlord may be able to pass on the cost of the work(s).

Tenants' rights to make improvements to a property

Unlike carrying out repairs the tenant will not normally have the right to insist that the landlord make actual alterations to the home. However, a tenant needs the following amenities and the law states that you should have:

- Bath or shower.
- Wash hand basin.
- Hot and cold water in each bath, basin, or shower.
- An indoor toilet.

If these amenities do not exist, then the tenant can contact the council's Environmental Health Officer. An improvement notice can be served on the landlord ordering him to put the amenity in.

Disabled tenants

If a tenant is disabled, he/she may need special items of equipment in the accommodation. The local authority may help in providing and, occasionally, paying for these.

The tenant will need to obtain the permission of the landlord. If you require more information, then contact the social services department locally.

Gas safety

The Gas safety (Installation and use) Regulations 1998
The Gas Cooking Appliances (safety) Regulations 1989
Heating Appliances (Fireguard) (safety) Regulations 1991
Gas Appliances (Safety) Regulations 1995

All the above are because the supply of gas and the appliances in a dwelling are safe. A Gas Safety certificate is required to validate this.

Furniture Safety

Furniture and Furnishings (Fire) (Safety) Regulations 1988 and 1993 (as amended)

Landlords and lettings agents are included in these regulations. The regulations set high standards for fire resistance for domestic upholstered furniture and other products containing upholstery. The main provisions are:

- Upholstered articles (i.e., beds, sofas, armchairs etc) must have fire resistant filling material.
- Upholstered articles must have passed a match resistant test or, if of certain kinds (such as cotton or silk) be used with a fire resistant interliner.
- The combination of the cover fabric and the filling material must have passed a cigarette resistance test.

The landlord should inspect property for non-compliant items before letting and replace with compliant items.

Electrical Safety
Electrical Equipment (Safety) Regulations 1994
Plugs and Sockets etc. (Safety) Regulations 1994.
The Electrical Equipment Regulations came into force in January 1995. Both sets of regulations relate to the supply of electrical equipment designed with a working voltage of between 50- and 1000-volts ac. (or between 75- and 1000-volts dc.). The regulations cover all the mains voltage household electrical goods including cookers, kettles, toasters, electric blankets, washing machines, immersion heaters etc.

The regulations do not apply to items attached to land. This is generally considered to exclude the fixed wiring and built-in appliances (e.g., central heating systems) from the regulations. Lettings agents and landlords should take the following action:

Essential:
Check all electrical appliances in all managed properties on a regular fixed term basis. Remove unsafe items and keep a record of checks.

Recommended:
- Have appliances checked by a qualified electrical engineer
- Avoid purchasing second hand electrical items
- There is no specific requirement for regular testing under the regulations. However, it is recommended that a schedule of checks, say on an annual basis, is put in place.

The availability of grants
There are several grants available to landlords at any one time. These will enable improvements to take place to a property. One of the main grants is the Disabled Facilities Grant. However, there are more, and your local authority can tell you what is available.

Regulations on Smoke and Carbon Monoxide detectors
From October 2015, all landlords, regardless of whether public or private sector, are required to install working smoke and carbon monoxide alarms in their properties, on each floor. The carbon

monoxide alarms will need to be placed in high-risk areas, i.e., where there are gas appliances. Carbon monoxide detectors will not be required in properties where there are no gas or solid fuel appliances.

A civil penalty of up to £5,000 will apply to landlords who fail to comply with this legislation.

Sanitation health and hygiene
Local authorities have a duty to serve an owner with a notice requiring the provision of a WC when a property has insufficient sanitation, sanitation meaning toilet waste disposal. They will also serve notice if it is thought that the existing sanitation is inadequate and is harmful to health or is a nuisance. Local authorities have similar powers under various Public Health Acts to require owners to put right bad drains and sewers, also food storage facilities and vermin, plus the containing of disease.

The Environmental Health Department, if it considers the problem bad enough will serve a notice requiring the landlord to put the defect right. In certain cases, the local authority can do the work and require the landlord to pay for it. This is called work in default.

****

CHAPTER 10

HOUSES IN MULTIPLE-OCCUPATION

A house in multiple-occupation – commonly known as an HMO – is a property which is rented by three or more tenants who aren't part of the same household (i.e., a family). Many landlords let HMOs as they consider them a more efficient way to run a rental portfolio. Although there may be more work to do, the opportunity to collect rent from a higher number of tenants and a potential higher rental yield is appealing. What's more, certain properties and locations are tailor-made for HMOs. For example, a busy student area with large, extendable properties. When it comes to tenants, HMOs are sometimes preferable due to potentially lower rent payments and the opportunity to live with more people.

As landlords have had to deal with increased regulation and financial setbacks in recent years, such as Section 24 and the 3% stamp duty surcharge, many have looked for ways to maximise the potential of their portfolios. Alongside incorporation, one of the most popular strategies has been to convert rental properties into HMOs in order to benefit from higher yields and rental returns.

Converting a property into an HMO

If you're considering converting a property into an HMO, there are several things you'll need to do, from meeting legal requirements to making the property habitable for more people.

HMO Licensing

One of the most important legal aspects of letting an HMO is getting the relevant licence in place. In the last few years, there have been many instances of landlords being issued with hefty fines for not complying with the law.

The rules surrounding HMO licensing were updated in October 2018. These rules state that If you're letting an HMO, it's highly likely you'll need some sort of licence. If your property is let to five or more tenants from more than one household, some or all the tenants share toilet, bathroom, or kitchen facilities and at least one tenant pays rent, then your property will be considered as a large HMO and will need a licence. HMO licences are valid for five years at a time and you'll require a separate licence for each HMO you're running.

As well as applying for a licence, there are various other compliance measures you'll need to meet. These include sending a valid gas safety certificate to your local authority each year, installing the relevant smoke alarms and carbon monoxide detectors, and having safety certificates for electrical appliances available on request.

HMO Minimum Room Sizes

At the same time as the licensing changes, guidelines for minimum HMO room sizes were also introduced with landlords needing to adhere to the following guidelines:

- Obligation to notify the local housing authority of any room in the HMO with a floor area of less than 4.64 square meters.
- ensure that the floor area of any room in the HMO used as sleeping accommodation by one person aged over 10 years is not less than 6.51 square meters.
- Ensure that the floor area of any room in the HMO used as sleeping accommodation by two persons aged over 10 years is not less than 10.22 square meters.
- Ensure that the floor area of any room in the HMO used as sleeping accommodation by one person aged under 10 years is not less than 4.64 square meters.
- Ensure that any room in the HMO with a floor area of less than 4.64 square meters is not used as sleeping accommodation.
- As part of these regulations, there were also new rules on overcrowding for landlords to comply with:

- Where any room in the HMO is used as sleeping accommodation by persons aged over 10 years only, it is not used as such by more than the maximum number of persons aged over 10 years specified in the license.
- Where any room in the HMO is used as sleeping accommodation by persons aged under 10 years only, it is not used as such by more than the maximum number of persons aged under 10 years specified in the license.
- Where any room in the HMO is used as sleeping accommodation by persons aged over 10 years and persons aged under 10 years, it is not used as such by more than the maximum number of persons aged over 10 years specified in the license.
- Depending on your local authority, there may be other criteria for you to meet to let a compliant HMO.

Does your property need converting to a HMO?

If your property is not HMO-ready, you may need to make some adjustments to make it suitable for three or more tenants from separate households.

Always remember the HMO property needs to be habitable and provide enough space for tenants to live comfortably. As well as your compliance obligations outlined above, the key things you'll need to consider are space, layout, facilities, furniture, and appliances. If you convert your property into an HMO, it will be visited by your local authority within five years. They will carry out a Housing Health and Safety Rating System (HHSRS) risk assessment to identify any issues.

It's worth noting, however, that the HHSRS was reviewed by the Government in 2019 and therefore its guidelines could be updated in the future. If any unacceptable risks – such as asbestos, carbon monoxide or radiation - are found during the assessment, you will need to address them immediately.

HMO Room conversions

It's likely you'll be converting the use of some rooms. For example, spare rooms may be converted to additional bathrooms and reception rooms to additional bedrooms. You may also need to move or construct walls to alter room sizes - these are all aspects you'll need to plan carefully before undertaking any work. It's also advisable to use a professional when working on the more significant parts of the conversion.

Also determine whether you need planning permission for any major renovations. Converting the garage into additional living space is another popular conversion option for HMO landlords. The likelihood is this will need planning permission, so again you'll need to check with your local council before undertaking any work. In many cases, traditional Victorian terraced houses and similar properties are ideal for HMO conversion. This is due to their spaciousness and the size of the reception rooms.

For example, in a three-bedroom terraced house a landlord could convert one reception room and the loft into bedrooms to turn it into a five-bedroom HMO. Converting reception rooms is often essential, but not always the right decision.

In the perfect scenario, the property will have two reception rooms - one of which can be converted, leaving the other room to remain as a dining or living space. Some renters might be put off properties with no living room or reception space, so it's something you'll need to consider carefully. Depending on the property, converting it into an HMO is going to be expensive and take some time. You need to make sure you budget properly and don't expect instant financial returns. Five quick HMO renovation tips:

- Remember your outdoor space - You may be tempted to focus on the interior of the property, but any outdoor space is equally important if you want your HMO to appeal to long-term tenants who are looking for a home. Seating and BBQ areas are likely to be popular with the modern renter.
- Prioritize kitchens and bathrooms - These enduringly popular rooms could be the dealbreaker when it comes to renters choosing your property. Tenants' expectations are likely to be high, so make sure you furnish to a high standard and add some nice touches such as an electric towel rail.

- Don't skimp on important features - while you'll want to keep costs down as much as possible, there is no point on being cheap when it comes to important features such as fridges, ovens, sofas, and beds.
- This approach will only end up costing you more in the long term.
- Maximize your space - If you've got tenants from three or more separate households in your property, you need to make it as spacious as possible. There are plenty of interior design tricks and tips out there to help you make the home feel more spacious without huge material changes.
- Be 100% ready to let - Tenants don't want to be moving into a building site and it's important you have everything finished before they move in to reduce the chances of damage or problems early in the tenancy.

HMO safety requirements

While converting your property to make it suitable for multiple tenants to live in, there are also a range of additional safety requirements you'll need to follow to let a compliant HMO. Fire safety will be one of your principal considerations. You will need to install smoke alarms, keep them in working order and be able to provide your local authority with a declaration of their safe condition on request. Alongside this, as with all lets, you'll need to ensure that all gas appliances are maintained, with a Gas Safe registered engineer carrying out a gas safety check each year.

All electrical installations and appliances you provide will need to be safe to use, while any furniture and furnishing you provide must meet the fire resistance regulations. Meanwhile, you will need an Electrical Installation Condition Report (EICR) and test certificates for your electrical appliances. It's likely you'll also need to install fire doors in certain places - make sure that your tenants know not to obstruct them or prop them open.

What's more, you'll need to keep all exits clear from obstructions (and advise tenants to do so too), while marking fire exits and providing tenants with instructions on what to do in the event of a fire. Some other safety requirements you'll need to consider when preparing your HMO to let could include:

- Locks for each bedroom (preferably thumb turn locks)
- Emergency lighting for fire safety
- Keeping pest control treatment records

The safety requirements for HMOs are very extensive and are likely to differ depending on your local authority. Therefore, it's always best to check with them first to get a full list of safety requirements before embarking on your conversion plans.

Houses in Multi-Occupation

What else do you need to consider when creating a HMO?
Fitness for human habitation
Another piece of legislation landlords need to comply with - including those letting HMOs - is the Homes (Fitness for Human Habitation) Act 2018, which came into force in March 2019.

The legislation means all rented accommodation must be suitable for human habitation at the start of the tenancy and throughout. It also provides tenants with greater powers to hold their landlord to account if their property is substandard.

To ensure your property is fit for human habitation, there are a range of potential issues you'll need to avoid. Some of these include:
- damp
- ventilation
- overcrowding
- drainage
- water supply

What's more, if the property contains any of the 29 hazards outlined in the HHSRS regulations, it's likely to be deemed unfit for human habitation by the courts. As a landlord, you'll be exempt from 'acts of God' and any issues caused by tenants.

One of the key differences between an HMO and a standard rental property is that you could encounter a higher turnover of tenants. Therefore, it's advisable to put aside at least two months' worth of rent each year to cover potential void periods.

You'll also need to make sure you have all the right tenancy documentation in place and an efficient referencing process for new tenants.

Property damage

Another crucial factor to remember is that, due to the nature of having more tenants, the property is likely to come under more stress over the course of a tenancy. Bathrooms, kitchens, floors, and doors will all take a lot more wear and so you need to make sure you're ready for this and are prepared to respond to all reasonable repair requests with speed and efficiency – as with any other tenancy. Be sure to check that your landlord insurance policy, if you have one, is suitable for a HMO – as not all landlord insurance policies cover a house of multiple-occupancy.

Buy-to-let mortgage terms for HMOs

When preparing to let an HMO, you'll need to check your buy-to-let mortgage terms. Not all agreements allow properties to be let as HMOs, so check your terms and conditions.

If you're not sure about something, you can check-in with your lender or speak to a buy-to-let mortgage broker. Your agreement may allow you to get started right away or you may need to arrange a different type of mortgage to proceed.

Research and budgeting

As mentioned above, you'll need to prepare the property fully before letting it, taking no shortcuts, and making sure you have enough money put aside to cover maintenance costs during and after the tenancy.

Converting a rental property to an HMO can be an effective investment with highly profitable rental yields, but it does require more work and upkeep.

Therefore, before jumping straight in, you'll need to do your research, take your time, and carefully compare the additional work and expense against the additional profit you're likely to make.

As with all projects of this nature, a considered combination of research and budgeting can help you to make the right decisions and ultimately benefit from the greater yields on offer from HMO properties.

Tenant refunds if rules are not followed

Renters could be due a refund of 12 months' rent if their landlord has not properly licenced the property they are living in. According to UK housing law, if landlords are renting a single property to multiple residents they need to licence the property with the local council.

The council can then check if the property meets the right standards for multiple occupancies. Other types of rental property may also have to be licensed under local council rules.

If a landlord hasn't licensed a rental property properly then tenants could be owed a refund through a rent repayment order (RRO) which could amount to a few thousand pounds. A tenant or the council can apply for this through a tribunal, and a council might offer help doing this as they run the licencing scheme.

If a tenant is to do this there most likely will be fees involved, however, these fees can be claimed back if the tenant are successful. The amount a tenant would get back depends on how much rent they pay.

If the rent for the entire property is £750, then a tenant could be entitled to a refund for the entire year which would equate to £9000, if the landlord is ordered by the tribunal to repay the entire amount.

If a tenant receives Housing Benefit for rent or have used Universal Credit to pay their rent then this can be reclaimed from the landlord by the council or the Department for Work and Pensions (DWP).

If a landlord does not have an HMO licence, then alongside having to repay rent, they cannot evict tenants from the property with a section 21 notice or "no-fault eviction" notice and they can

be banned from renting out properties. Tenants can also apply for a rent repayment order if:
- The landlord has not complied with a council notice
- The tenant has been harassed or evicted without the correct paperwork.

****

CHAPTER 11

TAKING BACK POSSESSION OF YOUR PROPERTY AFTER THE TENANCY ENDS OR BEFORE THE TENANCY ENDS

Note that the procedures for taking back possession are different in Scotland and Northern Ireland. For advice on evictions in Northern Ireland go to:
https://www.housingadviceni.org/advice-landlords/right-evict.
For Scotland go to: https://www.mygov.scot/ending-a-tenancy-as-a-landlord

Also, see the information about changes in Wales from July 2022 at the end of this chapter.

Fast-track (accelerated) possession
Previously, a landlord will have served a section 21 notice on the tenant at the start of the tenancy. However, following the passage of the Deregulation Act 2015, the landlord can no longer do this and must serve the notice after the tenant has been in occupation for

four months. This brings the tenancy to an end on the day of expiry, i.e., on the day of expiry of the six-month period, or 12-month period, whichever is appropriate. It should be noted that if a landlord takes a deposit from the tenant, then every deposit must be registered with the appropriate deposit service before the landlord can serve the s21 notice.

For all AST's issued after October 1st, 2015, a Form 6a is served. On expiry of the notice, if it is the landlord's intention to take possession of the property then the tenants should leave. It is worthwhile writing a letter to the tenants one month before expiry reminding them that they should leave. In the event of the tenant refusing to leave, then the landlord must then follow a process termed 'fast track possession'. This entails filling in the appropriate forms (N5B) which can be accessed from: www.gov.uk/accelerated-possession-eviction. The process is online and costs £355 (2024/2025). If a valid form 6 notice has been served on the tenant, the accelerated possession proceedings can begin, and the forms completed online which are then lodged with the court dealing with the area where the property is situated. To grant the accelerated possession order the court will require the following:

- The assured shorthold agreement
- The section 21 notice (or form 6a notice)
- Evidence of service of the notice

Taking Back Possession of a Property

The best form of service for the notice is by hand. If the notice has already been served, then evidence that the tenant has received it will be required. A copy must also be served on the tenant. This will be carried out by the court, although it might help if the landlord also serves a copy informing the tenant that they are taking proceedings. If the tenant disputes the possession proceedings in any way, they will have 14 days to reply to the court. If the case is well founded and the paperwork is in order, then there should be no case for defense.

Once the accelerated possession order has been granted then this will need to be served on the tenant, giving them 14 days to vacate. In certain circumstances, if the tenant pleads hardship the court can grant extra time to leave, six weeks as opposed to two weeks. If they still do not vacate, then an application will need to be made to court for a bailiff's warrant to evict the tenants. An accelerated possession order remains in force for six years from the date it was granted.

Going to court to end the tenancy
There may come a time when the landlord needs to go to court to regain possession of a property. This will usually arise when the contract has been breached by the tenant, for non-payment of rent or for some other breach such as nuisance or harassment. As we

have seen, a tenancy can be ended in a court on one of the grounds for possession.

However, as the tenancy will usually be an assured shorthold then it is necessary to consider whether the landlord is able to give two months notice and withhold the deposit, as opposed to going to court. The act of withholding the deposit will entail the landlord refusing to authorize the payment to the tenant online. This then brings arbitration into the frame. Deposit schemes have an arbitration system as an integral part of the scheme.

If the landlord decides, for whatever reason, to go to court, then any move to regain the property for breach of agreement will commence in the county court in the area in which the property is. The first steps in ending the tenancy will necessitate the serving of a notice of seeking possession using one of the Grounds for Possession detailed earlier in the book. If the tenancy is protected then 28 days must be given, the notice must be in prescribed form and served on the tenant personally (preferably).

If the tenancy is an assured shorthold, which is more often the case now, then 14 days' notice of seeking possession can be used. In all cases the ground to be relied upon must be clearly outlined in the notice.

If the case is more complex, then this will entail a particulars of claim being prepared, usually by a solicitor, as opposed to a standard possession form.

Taking Back Possession of a Property

A fee is paid when sending the particulars to court, which should be checked with the local county court. The standard form which the landlord uses for routine rent arrears cases is called the N119 and the accompanying summons is called the N5. Both forms can be obtained from the court or from:

justice.gov.uk/HMCTS/FormFinder.do.

When completed, the forms should be sent in duplicate to the county court and a copy retained for the landlord. The court will send a copy of the particulars of claim and the summons to the tenant. They will send the landlord a form which gives him a case number and court date to appear, known as the return date. On the return date, the landlord will arrive at court at least 15 minutes early. The landlord can represent his/her-self in simple cases but will be advised to use a solicitor for more contentious cases. If the tenant is present, then they will have a chance to defend themselves.

Several orders are available. However, if a landlord has gone to court on the mandatory ground eight then if the fact is proved then they will get possession immediately. If not, then the judge can grant an order, suspended whilst the tenant finds time to pay. In a lot of cases, it is more expedient for a landlord to serve notice-requiring possession, if the tenancy has reached the end of the period, and then wait two months before the property is regained.

This saves the cost and time of going to court particularly if the ground is one of nuisance or other, which will involve solicitors.

If the landlord regains possession of A property midway through the contractual term, then he will have to complete the possession process by use of bailiff, pay a fee and fill in another form, Warrant for Possession of Land. Take note that in Wales Tenants will be guaranteed minimum 12 **months occupancy from July 2022.** July 2022's implementation of the new Renting Homes (Wales) Act 2016 will increase the minimum notice period landlords must give tenants in order to regain possession of their property to six months.

What's more, landlords won't be able to serve notice during the first six months of the tenancy, and they won't be able to serve notice during the fixed term. Often referred to as a 'no fault eviction', these requirements combined have the effect of guaranteeing tenants a minimum 12-month occupancy where a six-month contract is signed (or 18 months with a 12-month contract), which is particularly relevant to landlords thinking of selling or moving back in soon.

Landlords who may be tempted to respond to a legitimate request for a repair by issuing a possession notice – commonly known as a 'retaliatory eviction' – will no longer be entitled to possession if the Court believes the notice was issued to avoid carrying out the repair. In this scenario, landlords won't be able to serve another 'no fault' notice for at least six months.

Changes to break clauses

For landlords in the habit of inserting a break clause into their tenancies, they'll only now be allowed where the tenancy is for a fixed term of two or more years.

Furthermore, a landlord won't be able to activate a break clause until at least 18 months into the contract, using a minimum six months' notice.

What about problematic tenants?

The Act offers some reassurance to landlords with tenants who have breached the terms of their tenancy. In these instances, the minimum notice is one month, though it can be less if the breach relates to anti-social behavior or there are serious rent arrears. However, as ever, if a tenant wishes to stand firm and remain in the property, a court order will have to be obtained to regain possession correctly and safely.

Serving notice won't be possible unless compliant. Landlords who fail to comply with certain obligations, such as registering the deposit within the correct timeframe or registering/obtaining a license through Rent Smart Wales, will be unable to serve such eviction notices, which will cause unwanted complications in regaining possession of their property.

For further detailed information on repossessing a property you should go to:

https://www.gov.uk/evicting-tenants/possession-hearings-and-orders

This site is particularly good and includes details of forms and costs.

****

CHAPTER 12

PRIVATE TENANCIES IN SCOTLAND

The law governing the relationship between private landlords and tenants in Scotland is different to that in England. Since the beginning of 1989, new private sector tenancies in Scotland were covered by the Housing (Scotland) Act 1988. Following the passage of this Act, private sector tenants no longer had any protection as far as rent levels were concerned and tenants enjoyed less security of tenure. However, The **Private Housing (Tenancies) (Scotland) Act 2016**, passed by the Scottish Parliament and coming into force on 1st December 2017, changed the law concerning private tenancies in Scotland. The main provisions of the Act are outlined below.

(Please note that the Scottish Governments moratorium on rent increases and ban on serving s21 notices has now ended (March 2024)).

The Private Residential Tenancy
On 1 December 2017 a new type of tenancy came into force, called the private residential tenancy, it replaced assured and short assured tenancy agreements for all new tenancies from 1st

December 2017. because of passing of The Private Housing (Tenancies) (Scotland) Act 2016.

The new Scottish Private Residential Tenancy, (SPRT) delivers improved security of tenure for tenants, including students in smaller purpose built and mainstream private rented accommodation, and the power for local authorities to designate rent pressure zones within their jurisdiction. There is also a streamlined procedures for starting and ending a tenancy and a model agreement for landlords and tenants.

The SPRT is the standard tenancy agreement between residential landlords and tenants and replaced the most common types of residential tenancies in Scotland – the Short-Assured Tenancy and the Assured Tenancy.

What changes has the private residential tenancy brought in?
Any tenancy that started on or after 1 December 2017 will be a private residential tenancy.

These new tenancies brought in changes and improvements to the private rented sector, including:
- **No more fixed terms** - private residential tenancies are open ended, meaning a landlord can't ask a tenant to leave just because they have been in the property for 6 months as they can with a short, assured tenancy.

- **Rent increases** – a tenant's rent can only be increased once every 12 months (with 3 months' notice) and if they think the proposed increase is unfair, they can refer it to a rent officer.
- **Longer notice period** - if a tenant has lived in a property for longer than 6 months the landlord will have to give them at least 84 days notice to leave (unless they have broken a term in the tenancy).
- **Simpler notices** - the notice to quit process has been scrapped and replaced by a simpler notice to leave process.
- **Model tenancy agreement** - the Scottish Government have published a model private residential tenancy that can be used by landlords.

Person already an assured/short, assured tenant

If a tenant was already renting and were an assured or short assured tenant, on 1 December 2017, their tenancy will continue as normal until they or their landlord brings it to an end following the correct procedure. If a landlord, then offers a tenant a new tenancy this will be a private residential tenancy.

A private residential tenancy is one that meets the following conditions:

- the tenancy started on or after 1 December 2017
- it is let to a person as a separate dwelling (home)
- the person must be an individual, meaning not a company

- it's their main or only home
- they must have a lease (although a written agreement not needed for a lease to exist)
- the tenancy is not an exemptions tenancy, as listed below.

Tenancy agreements

A person has the right to a tenancy agreement, which can be either a written or electronic copy, within 28 days of the start of the tenancy. The Scottish Government has published a model tenancy that a landlord can use to set up a tenancy. This tenancy plus a set of notes that a landlord must give to the tenant can be accessed at www.mygov.scot/tenancy-agreement-scotland.

This tenancy agreement contains certain statutory terms that outline both parties' rights and obligations including:
- The tenant's and landlord/letting agent's contact details
- The address and details of the rented property
- The start date of the tenancy
- How much the rent is and how it can be increased
- How much the deposit is and information about how it will be registered
- Who is responsible for insuring the property?
- The tenant must inform the landlord when they are going to be absent from the property for more than 14 days

- The tenant will take reasonable care of the property
- The condition that the landlord must make sure the property is in, including the repairing standard.
- That the tenant must inform the landlord the need of any repairs.
- That the tenant will give reasonable access to the property, when the landlord has given at least 48 hours notice
- The process that the tenancy can be ended.

If a landlord uses the Scottish Government's' model tenancy, they should also give the tenant the 'Easy Read Notes' which will explain the tenancy terms in plain English. If a landlord does not use the model tenancy, they must give the tenant the private residential tenancy statutory terms: supporting notes, with their lease, which will explain the basic set of terms that a landlord has to include in the lease.

Rent Increases

The rent can only be increase once every 12 months and the landlord needs to give a tenant 3 months notice, using the correct notice of the rent increase. If the tenant doesn't agree to the rent increase, they can refer it to the local rent officer. The referral to the rent officer must be done within 21 days of receiving the rent increase notice. When a referral is made to the rent officer, they will first issue a provisional order which will suggest the amount the rent can be increased. The tenant will have 14 days from the date the provisional order is issued to request a reconsideration. If the tenant requests a reconsideration the rent officer will look at it again before making a final order and telling them the date that the increase will take place.

Ending a tenancy

If a tenant wants to end the tenancy, then they will have to give the landlord 28 days' notice in writing. The notice must state the day on which the tenancy is to end, normally the day after notice period has expired. The tenant can agree a different notice period with the landlord as long it is in writing. If there is no agreed notice, then 28 days' notice is the minimum required.

Landlord access

The tenant must allow reasonable access to the landlord to carry out repairs, inspections, or valuations when:
- the landlord has given at least 48 hours' written notice, or
- access is required urgently for the landlord to view or carry out works in relation to the repairing standard.

If a tenant refuses access the landlord can make an application to the First Tier Tribunal Housing and Property Chamber who may make an order allowing them access.

Getting repairs carried out

As with other tenancies, the landlord must keep the property wind and watertight, and in a condition that is safe to live in. The landlord is also responsible for making sure that the property repairing standard is met. This is a basic level of repair that is required by law. The landlord must give the tenant information on the repairing standard and what they can do if the property does not meet it.

If a tenant wants to carry out work on their home, such as redecorating or installing a second phone line, they will need to seek permission from the landlord. Some tenancy agreements will include a clause telling the tenant whether they can carry out this kind of work.

Can a tenant sublet or pass their tenancy on to someone else?

A tenant cannot sublet, take in a lodger, or pass their tenancy on to someone else before first getting written agreement from the landlord.

Tenancies that cannot be private residential tenancy

Almost all new private tenancies created on or after 1st December 2017 will be private residential tenancies. However, there are several exemptions, including the following:
- Tenancies at a low rent
- Tenancies of shops

- Licensed premises
- Tenancies of agricultural land
- Lettings to students (meaning purpose-built student accommodation)
- Holiday lettings
- Resident landlords
- Police Housing
- Military Housing
- Social Housing
- Sublet, assigned etc. social housing
- Homeless persons
- Persons on probation or released from prison etc.
- Accommodation for asylum seekers
- Displaced persons
- Shared ownership
- Tenancies under previous legislation
- Assured or short assured tenancies

Short assured and assured tenancies

Most residential lettings in Scotland made after 2 January 1989 and before 1st December 2017 are short, assured tenancies. Those that aren't short assured are normally assured tenancies.

Short, assured tenancies This was the most common type of tenancy. A short, assured tenancy makes it easier for a landlord to repossess a property than an assured tenancy.

Before any agreement is signed, a landlord must use form AT5 to tell new tenants that the tenancy will be a short, assured tenancy. If they don't, the tenancy will automatically be an assured tenancy.

Initially, a short, assured tenancy must be for 6 months or more. After the first 6 months, the tenancy can be renewed for a shorter period.

Assured tenancies

At the beginning of an assured tenancy, it will be classed as a 'contractual assured tenancy' for a fixed period. The tenancy automatically becomes a 'statutory assured tenancy' if:

- the landlord ends the tenancy by issuing a notice to quit (e.g., because they want to change the agreement) and the tenant stays in the property
- the fixed period covered by the tenancy comes to an end and the tenant stays in the property.

There are different rights and responsibilities on both landlord and tenant depending on the type of assured tenancy.

Other types of tenancy

Most tenancies in Scotland issued before December 2017 are short assured or assured tenancies.

The other tenancy types are:
- 'common law' tenancy - if a tenant shares their home as a lodger
- regulated tenancy - the most common form of tenancy before 1989
- agricultural tenancy
- crofting tenancy

'Common law' tenancies

If a landlord is sharing their house or flat with their tenants, they can't use the short assured or assured tenancy. Instead, they will automatically have what is known as a 'common law tenancy'. The tenant doesn't have to have a written contract, but the landlord may use a lodger agreement to create a contract between them and the tenant - so both are clear about what has been agreed.

Regulated tenancies

Tenancies created before 2 January 1989 are generally regulated tenancies. As not many exist, we will not be describing them further here.

Agricultural tenancies

There are 3 types of agricultural tenancy:

- limited duration tenancy - if the lease is for more than 5 years
- short, limited duration tenancy - if the lease is for 5 years or less
- 1991 Act tenancy - if the tenancy began before 2003

All agricultural tenants have the right to:
- a written lease
- compensation at the end of the tenancy for any improvements they made to the land during their tenancy
- leave the tenancy to a spouse or relative in their will
- If the lease is over 5 years, agricultural tenants can also:
- pass their tenancy on to a relative or spouse within their lifetime
- use the land for non-agricultural purposes
- Tenants with a 1991 Act tenancy have the right to buy the land they are leasing.

If there's a house on the land, both landlord and tenant have obligations to keep it in good repair.

Crofting tenancies

Crofting is a system of landholding unique to the Highlands and Islands of Scotland. Usually, the crofter holds the croft on the 'statutory conditions' and doesn't have a written lease. Crofting is regulated by the Crofting Commission. The tenant must get written agreement from the Commission if you want to make any changes to a crofting tenancy (including a change of tenant).

What the landlord must include in a tenancy agreement
If a landlord used an assured or short assured tenancy, the agreement must be written down. It must include:
- the names of all people involved
- the rental price and how it's paid
- the deposit amount and how it will be protected (see below)
- when the deposit can be fully or partly withheld (eg to repair damage caused by tenants)
- the property address
- the start and end date of the tenancy
- any tenant or landlord obligations
- who's responsible for minor repairs
- which bills your tenants are responsible for
- a statement telling the tenant that antisocial behaviour is a breach of the agreement

For other types of tenancy, it's still good practice to put the agreement in writing, including other information. To avoid any confusion later, the landlord can include other information in the agreement, such as:

- whether the tenancy can be ended early and how this can be done
- information on how and when the rent will be reviewed
- whether the property can be let to someone else (sublet) or have lodgers

Changes to tenancy agreements

The landlord must get the agreement of their tenants if they want to make changes to the terms of their tenancy agreement.

Preventing discrimination

Unless the landlord has a very strong reason, they must change anything in a tenancy agreement that might discriminate against tenants on the grounds of:

- gender
- sexual orientation
- disability (or because of something connected with their disability)
- religion or belief
- being a transsexual person
- the tenant being pregnant or having a baby

Ending a Short-assured tenancy

To get a property back, the landlord must give tenants:

- A 'notice to quit' and a 'Section 33 notice'.
- For a short-assured tenancy, the minimum notice period is 40 days if the tenancy is for 6 months or longer.
- For a tenancy that is continuing on a month-by-month basis after the original period has ended, the notice period is a minimum of 28 days.
- The landlord must give 2 months notice when giving a Section 33 notice.
- They can issue both the notice to quit and Section 33 notice at the same time.

Other tenancy types (excluding the new private residential tenancy)
For other tenancy types the landlord must give at least:

- 28 days if the tenancy is for up to 1 month
- 31 days if the tenancy is for up to 3 months
- 40 days if the tenancy is for more than 3 months

Ending a tenancy early
A landlord can end a tenancy early if the tenant breaks a condition of the tenancy agreement orlandlord and tenant agree to end the tenancy

If tenants don't leave

If the notice period expires and tenants don't leave the property, the landlord can start the process of eviction through the courts. A landlord must tell tenants of their intention to get a court order by giving them a 'notice of intention to raise proceedings' (AT6) (see appendix).

If tenants want to leave

The tenancy agreement should say how much notice tenants need to give before they can leave the property. If the notice isn't mentioned in the tenancy agreement, the minimum notice a tenant can give is:

- 28 days if their tenancy runs on a month-to-month basis (or if it's for less than a month)
- 40 days if their tenancy is for longer than 3 months

Ending a tenancy early

Unless there's a break clause in the tenancy agreement, a landlord can insist that their tenants pay rent until the end of the tenancy. If tenants leave the property without giving notice, or before the notice has run out, they're still responsible for the property and the rent by law.

Houses in multiple occupation (HMOs)

If a tenant is living in a bedsit, shared flat, lodging, shared house, hostel or bed and breakfast accommodation it's likely that they will be living in a house in multiple occupation. A landlord will have an HMO if:

- tenants live with two or more other people, and
- they don't belong to the same family, and
- they share some facilities, e.g., a bathroom or kitchen, and
- the accommodation is their only or main home (if they are a student, their term-time residence counts as their main home).

If they live with a homeowner their family doesnt count as 'qualifying persons' when deciding whether a property is an HMO.

So, for example, if they share accommodation with the owner and one other unrelated lodger, they won't live in an HMO. If they live with the owner and two other unrelated lodgers, they will live in an HMO.

Before the council gives a landlord an HMO licence, it will carry out the following checks:

Is the landlord a fit and proper person to hold a licence?

Before it will grant an HMO licence, the council must check that the owner and anyone who manages the property (for example, a letting agent) don't have any criminal convictions, for example, for fraud or theft.

Is the property managed properly?
The council must check that the landlord respects tenants' legal rights. They should be given a written tenancy agreement stating clearly what the landlord's responsibilities are, and what the tenants responsibilities are. This should cover things like rent, repairs, and other rules. To manage the property properly. The landlord must:
- keep the property and any furniture and fittings in good repair
- deal with the tenant fairly and legally when it comes to rent and other payments, for example they:
- must go through the correct procedure if they want to increase the rent
- cannot resell the tenant gas or electricity at a profit
- not evict the tenant illegally
- make sure that their tenants don't annoy or upset other people living in the area.

Does the property meet the required standards?
To meet the standards expected of an HMO property:

- the rooms must be a decent size, for example, every bedroom should be able to accommodate a bed, a wardrobe, and a chest of drawers.
- there must be enough kitchen and bathroom facilities for the number of people living in the property, with adequate hot and cold-water supplies.
- adequate fire safety measures must be installed, for example the landlord must provide smoke alarms and self-closing fire doors.
- make sure there is an emergency escape route.
- all gas and electrical appliances must be safe.
- heating, lighting, and ventilation must all be adequate.
- the property should be secure, with good locks on the doors and windows. There must be a phone line installed so that tenants can set up a contract with a phone company to supply the service.

What are the landlord's responsibilities?

To keep their HMO licence, a landlord must maintain the property properly:

- **Common parts** - these must be kept clean and in good repair (for example, the stairwell, hall, shared kitchen, and bathroom). However, the landlord can include a clause in the tenancy agreement which passes this responsibility onto the tenants.

- **Shared facilities** - these should be kept in good repair (for example, the cooker, boiler, fridge, sinks, bath, and lighting)
- **Heating, hot water and ventilation** - these facilities must all be kept in good order
- **Gas safety** - all gas appliances and installations must be safe (for example, a gas fire, boiler or cooker) - these should be checked once a year by a Gas Safe Register engineer
- **Electrical safety-** all electrical appliances and installations must be safe - these should be tested every three years by a contractor approved by the National Inspection Council for Electrical Installation Contracting (NICEIC) or SELECT, Scotland's trade association for the electrical, electronics and communications systems industry
- **Fire precautions** - all fire precautions (for example, smoke alarms and fire extinguishers) must be in good working order and that the fire escape route is kept safe and free from obstructions.
- **Furniture** - all furniture supplied must meet safety standards (for example, isn't flammable)
- **Roof, windows, and exterior** - these must all be adequately maintained
- **Rubbish** - enough rubbish bins must be provided

- **Deposits** - tenants deposits must be returned within a reasonable time when they move out, preferably within 14 days.

The landlord should also put-up notices in the accommodation giving the name and address of the person responsible for managing it so that the tenant can contact them whenever necessary and explaining what the tenant should do in an emergency, for example if there is a gas leak or a fire.

Tenants' responsibilities:
- **Repairs** – the tenant should let the landlord know if anything in the property needs repairing, particularly if this is something they are responsible for keeping in good order, such as the roof, boiler, or toilet
- **Damage** – the tenant must take good care of the property and try not to damage anything
- **Rubbish** - not let rubbish pile up in or around the property but dispose of it properly in the bins provided
- **Inspections** - let the landlord inspect the property so they can check whether any maintenance work needs doing. Normally this should happen once every six months.
- The landlord must give 24 hours' written notice before coming round.

- **Behave responsibly** - make sure that the tenant doesnt behave in a way that can annoy or upset neighbours. The landlord is responsible for dealing with any complaints made by neighbors and must act if they are unhappy with tenants' behavior.

Safeguarding Tenancy Deposits

A tenancy deposit scheme is a scheme provided by an independent third party to protect deposits until they are due to be repaid. Three schemes are now operating:
- Letting Protection Service Scotland
- Safedeposits Scotland
- Mydeposits Scotland

Landlord's legal duties

The legal duties on landlords who receive a tenancy deposit are:
- to pay deposits to an approved tenancy deposit scheme
- to provide the tenant with key information about the tenancy and deposit

Further details about the individual schemes are available on the individual scheme web sites below.

Email addresses and telephone numbers are also included. All three schemes have a range of information available for both landlords (and their agents) as well as tenants and these include how landlords can join the schemes, how to submit deposits, how to ask for repayment of deposits and how the dispute resolution service will work.

Letting Protection Service Scotland

www.lettingprotectionscotland.com

Address:

The Pavilions

Bridgwater Road

Bristol BS99 6BN

Email contact: events@lettingprotectionscotland.com

Telephone: 0330 303 0031

SafeDeposits Scotland

www.safedepositsscotland.com

Address:

Lower Ground

250 West George Street

Glasgow

G2 4QY

Email contact: info@safedepositsscotland.com

Telephone: 03333 213 136

Mydeposits Scotland
www.mydepositsscotland.co.uk
Address:
Premiere House
Elstree Way
Borehamwood
Hertfordshire
WD6 1JH
Email contact: info@mydepositsscotland.co.uk
Telephone: 0333 321 9402

****

CHAPTER 13

MANAGING THE FINANCES-TAX AND OTHER ISSUES

Capital Gains Tax (CGT) on buy to let property

If you sell the property for more than you paid for it after deducting costs such as stamp duty and estate agent/solicitors' fees you will be liable for CGT. By making a profit, you are essentially 'gaining capital', and so the tax applies. However, as an individual you get an annual allowance to set against any gain. In the 2023/2024 tax year, this allowance is £6,000 and £3,000 for trusts. This has further reduced to £3,000 and £1500 in 2024/25. This is a special allowance purely for capital items and is separate from the annual personal income tax allowance. If the gain is greater than the £3,000 allowance, you will pay tax at a rate of either 18% or 28% on that profit depending on the amount of income and capital gains you have.

There are legitimate ways to reduce the amount of Capital Gains Tax (CGT) payable:

- A loss made on the sale of a buy to let property in previous years
- Solicitor fees
- Estate agent fees
- Costs of advertising the property for sale
- Stamp duty
- Any expenditure on 'capital' items

These expenses can be deducted from your capital gain. There are also certain tax reliefs available. For example, if the property was previously your main residence, the gain may be reduced.

Like income tax, any gain is declared on your Self Assessment tax return. The tax is therefore payable by the 31st of January in the year after the tax year in which the property was sold.

From April 2019, any tax payable on the profit of the sale of the property is payable within 60 days of the date the property is sold.

Tax on buy to let property income

The income you receive as rent is taxable. You need to declare any rent you receive as part of your Self Assessment tax return. The tax on your income is then charged in accordance with your income tax banding (20% for basic rate taxpayers, 40% for higher rate, and 45% for additional rate). However, you can minimise the tax you have to pay by deducting certain 'allowable expenses' from your taxable rental income.

Allowable expenses include:

- Some of the Interest on buy to let mortgages and other finance charges (but see below)
- Council tax, insurance, ground rents etc
- Property repairs and maintenance – however large improvements such as extensions etc will not be income tax deductible. They will be added to the cost of the property when it is sold and be deductible against any capital gain.
- Legal, management and other professional fees such as letting agency fees.
- Other property expenses including buildings insurance premiums

The 2015 Summer Budget reduced the amount of tax relief that is available for interest on buy to let mortgages from April 2017. Prior to April 2017, tax was payable on your net rental income after deducting allowable expenses including mortgage interest.

Changes to landlords' 'wear and tear allowance'

If the property or properties you let out are fully furnished, you used to be able to claim for wear and tear of furnishings, such as cookers, carpets, beds, and televisions. The wear and tear allowance allowed you to claim a maximum of 10% of the net annual rent (income less expenses) each year. However, this has now changed. The government now allows you to claim tax relief on anything you spend on replacing what it labels as a 'domestic item.' Crucially, this only applies to items you are replacing. You can't claim tax relief on the actual cost of kitting out a property for the first time with furniture or appliances.

It can only apply when an item is genuinely replaced and no longer used in the property.

What qualifies for the 'replacement of domestic items relief'?
The government lists several examples of what domestic items qualify for this new relief. These include:
- Replacement beds
- Replacement carpets
- Replacement crockery or cutlery
- Replacement curtains
- Replacement fridges, washing machines etc
- Replacement sofas

It's worth remembering that you can only claim for a like-for-like replacement. If, for example, you bought a new fridge worth £600, but the cost of replacing your old fridge with a very similar one was only £400, you'd only be able to claim £400 relief.

You can also claim for the cost of disposing items (usually electrical goods).

How does the 'replacement of domestic items relief' work?

You can deduct the cost of replacing domestic items from your rental income tax when calculating your net profit for the year, on which you pay tax.

So, say you replace a number of items in your property, ready for some new tenants. These include curtains for £200, a washing machine for £250 (which also costs £50 to dispose of) and a new bed for £400.

The total relief you can claim for is £200 + £250 + £50 + £400, which amounts to £900.

This can be deducted from your annual rental income to work out your tax bill at the end of the tax year.

Using a limited company to minimise tax

There is no simple answer to this. It depends on several factors such as how many properties you hold, whether you need the income quickly and how long you want to hold the properties for and your individual circumstances.

Limited companies are not affected by the Mortgage interest relief restriction. Interest for limited companies is classed as a business expense and fully deductible against income. Companies pay corporation tax at a fixed rate irrespective of the size of the profits. The Corporation Tax rate is currently at 25% in 2024/2025.

This makes the tax rate very attractive compared to 40% for higher rate taxpayers and 45% for additional higher rate taxpayers.

The question is how the money in the company is passed to the individual. If the money is taken out of the company as a dividend, only the first £1,000 of dividend income is tax free. Any dividends taken out more than this will either be charged at 7.5% for a basic rate taxpayer 32.5% for a higher rate taxpayer or 37.5% for an additional higher rate taxpayer. This tax is after the corporation tax at 25% has been paid.

The money could be taken as a salary; however, the company would have to operate PAYE and pay Employers National insurance contributions on any salaries paid. This usually in most circumstances works out more expensive than paying dividends. Companies also do not benefit from the annual allowance against capital gains. So, extracting the money for a sold buy to let property could be less tax efficient than holding the property as an individual. As you must pay the 25% corporation tax on any gain, no annual allowance is given and you must pay tax on extracting the money from the company, whereas even a higher rate taxpayer only pays 28% on any gain from the sale of a buy to let as an individual.

Companies also must prepare accounts to be filed with company's house, prepare and file corporation tax returns which can be more onerous than self-assessment returns.

Interest rates charged on mortgages to companies have historically been higher than to individuals so further investigation of the comparison of the rates charged should be considered alongside the tax implications.

Transferring a current buy to let property into a limited company can trigger stamp duty and capital gains tax charges at the time of transfer so advice should be sought before undertaking such a transaction. Due to the complexities of this area, it is essential that you seek proper professional advice.

Inheritance tax on a buy to let property

Inheritance Tax is payable on buy to let properties but the amount changes depending on your circumstances. A buy to let property that you own will form part of your estate for Inheritance Tax purposes. It works like this: if you're operating as a sole landlord – with the buy to let mortgage in your name as an individual and your estate entirely owned by you alone – then you're liable to inheritance tax if your property value less any outstanding mortgage (or combined value of your estate) exceeds £325,000. If you're in this with a married or civil partner, then you each have a threshold of £325,000 so the inheritance tax kicks in at £650,000. Anything above these amounts is taxed at 40%. Inheritance tax planning is complex and something that should be discussed with an expert tax or financial adviser.

Furnished holiday lets

Changes to the tax regime covering furnished holiday lettings

The situation concerning Furnished holiday lettings and tax, outlined below, covers the 2024/25 tax year. From April 2025 a new regime will be in place which places a greater tax burden on owners on FHL. The Chancellor has announced that the favourable tax treatment furnished holiday lettings (FHLs) currently benefit from will be abolished with effect from 6 April 2025. Currently, FHLs benefit from a range of beneficial tax rules including:

- The full amount of finance costs (i.e. mortgage interest) can be deducted from FHL income;
- On disposal of an FHL, business asset disposal relief may be available which results in a 10% capital gains tax rate applying;
- Profits from FHLs count as relevant earnings for pension purposes meaning tax-advantaged pension contributions can be made;
- Where the accruals basis applies, capital allowances on items such as furniture and fixtures and fittings can be claimed against the rental income; and
- Where the cash basis applies, expenditure on furniture etc. is generally deductible as an expense of the property business.

Managing the Finances-Tax and Other Issues

The current rules concerning furnished holiday lets (2024)
What are the 'Furnished Holiday Letting' Tax Rules?
For your holiday home to qualify and benefit from the tax rules governing furnished holiday lettings it must first meet all the following criteria:
- Your holiday home must be located within the European Economic Area (EEA).
- Your holiday home must be let on a commercial basis with a view to making a profit from the lettings.
- Your holiday home must be furnished.

The occupation requirements
There are also several occupation requirements your holiday home will need to meet:
- Your holiday home must be available for at least 210 days (30 weeks) in a 12-month period.
- Your holiday home must be let to the public as holiday accommodation for at least 105 days (15 weeks) in a 12-month period. If your holiday home is new and unable to hit this occupation level it will be taken into consideration.

If your holiday home is occupied by the same guests for more than 31 consecutive days, that 'longer term' form of occupation cannot add up to more than 155 days. This is within a 12-month period. If you own more than one holiday home, an average would be taken across all the qualifying properties meaning that if a single property fell beneath the required occupancy threshold it could potentially be buoyed up by other holiday homes that you own.

What if you have a bad year and don't meet the requirements?
To continue to qualify as Furnished Holiday Accommodation your holiday home will not need to meet the occupation requirements every year. You will be allowed to miss the thresholds for two consecutive years, with your holiday home ceasing to be qualify on the third year. This means that as a bear minimum, your holiday home will need to meet the entire occupation requirement at least once every three years.

The benefits of qualifying as Furnished Holiday Letting
There is a wide range of benefits associated with Furnished Holiday Letting Accommodation, which you should discuss with your accountant.

These benefits include: Profits from furnished holiday lets are deemed "relevant earnings", allowing for tax advantaged pension savings to be made that ordinary letting businesses do not qualify for. Capital allowances can be made on the capital expenditure you make on your holiday home. The first £200,000 of capital expenditure incurred by a person can qualify for 100% Capital Allowances (as at 2024). If you wish to sell your holiday home a range of Capital Gains Tax reliefs, usually only available to trading ventures, can be claimed. These could include Entrepreneurs' Relief, Roll-over Relief and Hold-over relief. Many holiday home businesses will be run by a husband-and-wife team. In this case profits can be allocated in any proportion required, irrespective of their actual shares in the ownership of the property.

A very useful website in relation to tax advantages and reliefs is: https://www.classic.co.uk/holiday-lets/tax-notes-for-furnished-holiday-lettings.

****

Useful Websites

The Buying Process
The Local Government Association
www.lga.gov.uk
Confederation of Scottish Local Authorities
www.cosla.gov.uk
Greater London Authority
www.london.gov.uk
The Environment Agency
www.environment-agency.gov.uk
www.homecheckuk.com

House Prices
Halifax www.halifax.co.uk
Nationwide www.nationwide.co.uk
Land Registry www.landreg.gov.uk
www.zoopla.co.uk
www.ourproperty.co.uk
www.upmystreet.com

Property search sites
www.hometrack.co.uk
www.rightmove.co.uk

www.zoopla.co.uk
www.fish4.co.uk
www.findaproperty.com
www.thisislondon.co.uk

The buying and selling process

The Law Society www.lawsoc.org.uk
The Council of Mortgage Lenders www.cml.org.uk
HM Customs and Revenue www.hmrc.gov

Scotland

Law Society of Scotland www.scotlaw.org.uk

Leasehold/freehold

Lease www.lease-advice.org
Association of Residential Managing Agents
www.arma.org.uk

Mortgage search sites/brokers

Money facts www.moneyfacts.co.uk
www.moneysupermarket.co.uk
www.moneynet.co.uk

New homes
NHBC www.nhbc.co.uk

Renting and Letting
UK Association of Letting Agents (UKALA)
Tel: 0330 055 3322 Website: www.ukala.org.uk

Specialist rental property sites
www.zoopla.co.uk
www.rightmove.co.uk

Auctions
www.propwatch.com
www.primelocation.com
www.bbc.co.uk/homes/property/buying_auction
www.propertyauctions.com

Sample tenancies and notices for Buy-to-Let properties
https://landlordknowledge.co.uk/landlord-forms

****

A SUMMARY OF IMPORTANT TERMS

FREEHOLDER: Someone who owns a property outright.

LEASEHOLDER: Someone who has been granted permission to live on someone else's land for a fixed term.

TENANCY: One form of lease, the most common types of which are fixed term or periodic.

LANDLORD: A person who owns the property in which the tenant lives.

LICENCE: A licence is an agreement entered into whereby the landlord is merely giving you permission to occupy his/her property for a limited period.

TRESPASSER: Someone who has no right through an agreement to live in a property.

PROTECTED TENANT: In the main, subject to certain exclusions, someone whose tenancy began before 15th January 1989.

ASSURED TENANT: In the main, subject to certain exclusions, someone whose tenancy began after 15th January 1989.

NOTICE TO QUIT: A legal document giving the protected tenant twenty-eight days' notice that the landlord intends to apply for possession of the property to the County Court.

GROUND FOR POSSESSION: One of the stated reasons for which the landlord can apply for possession of the property.

MANDATORY GROUND: Where the judge must give possession of the property.

DISCRETIONARY GROUND: Where the judge may or may not give possession, depending on his own opinion.

STUDENT LETTING: A tenancy granted by a specified educational institution.

HOLIDAY LETTING: A dwelling used for holiday purposes only.

ASSURED SHORTHOLD TENANCY: A fixed-term post-1989 tenancy.

PAYMENT OF RENT: Where you pay a regular sum of money in return for permission to occupy a property or land for a specified period of time.

FAIR RENT: A rent set by the Rent Officer every two years for most pre-1989 tenancies and is lower than a market rent.

MARKET RENT: A rent deemed to be comparable with other non-fair rents in the area.

RENT ASSESSMENT COMMITTEE: A committee set up to review rents set by either the Rent Officer or the landlord.

PREMIUM: A sum of money charged for permission to live in a property.

DEPOSIT: A sum of money held against the possibility of damage to property.

QUIET ENJOYMENT: The right to live peacefully in your own home.

REPAIRS: Work required to keep a property in good order.

IMPROVEMENTS: Alterations to a property.

LEGAL AID: Help with your legal costs, which is dependent on income.

HOUSING BENEFIT: Financial help with rent, which is dependent on income.

HOUSING ADVICE CENTRE: A center which exists to give advice on housing-related matters, and which is usually local authority-funded.

LAW CENTRE: A center which exists for the purpose of assisting the public with legal advice.

****

Index

Airbnb, 85
Amenity Land, 62
Assured shorthold tenancy, 100

Building Guarantees, 53
Building insurance, 68
Building Land, 61
Buildings in conservation areas, 52
Buy to Let Mortgages, 21
Buy-to-let investors, 60

Capital yields, 15
Commercial Investments, 61
Company lets, 78
Conveyancing, 27
Council tax, 111

Damages, 117
Deposit, 20, 87, 88, 94, 140
Deposits, 87, 88
Developers, 59
Disabled tenants, 119

Electrical Equipment (Safety) Regulations 1994, 120
Electrical Safety, 120
Ending a tenancy, 103
Energy Performance Certificates, 34, 36
Exchange of contracts, 55

Finance, 66
Financial Conduct Authority (FCA, 22
Flipping, 59
Forced sales, 59
Freehold, 97
Furniture, 91, 119

Garage blocks, 61
Gas Appliances(Safety) Regulations 1995, 119
Gas Cooking Appliances (safety) Regulations 1989, 119
Gas safety, 119
Gas safety (Installation and use) Regulations 1998, 119
Ground rents, 59

Heating Appliances(Fireguard) (safety) Regulations 1991, 119
Holiday lets, 83, 84
Houses in multiple occupation, 60

Industrial units, 61
Insurance, 93
Investment properties, 59
Investment properties, 15

Land Registry, 28, 180
Landlords obligations, 102
Leasehold, 93, 98, 181
Leasehold Reform Act 2024, 50
Legal pack, 65
Licenses, 101
Local authority properties, 59

Mixed Use Properties, 61
Mortgage, 66
Mortgage arrangement fees, 43
Moving into a property, 87

National House Building Council Guarantee (NHBCG), 54

Overcrowding, 105

Probate, 59
Property investors, 59
Protected tenancies, 100
Purchasing a flat, 47

Receivership sales, 59
Rental guarantees, 90
Rental yields, 15
Renters Reform Bill 2023, 7, 137
Repairs, 3, 115
Reporting repairs, 117
Repossessions, 58, 59
Residential Investments, 60
Retail shops, 61

Sanitation, 122
Scotland, 145
Service charges, 93
Services, 53, 92, 102
Special Conditions of Sale, 65
Stagflation, 6
Stamp Duty, 24

Structural surveys, 41
Student lets, 80

Tenancy Deposit Protection Scheme, 87
Tenanted Properties, 60
Tenants obligations, 102
The 1985 Landlord and Tenant Act, 92
The business plan, 17
The contract, 101
The National Energy Services Scheme, 53
The National House Building Council, 53
The public sector, 77
The tenancy agreement, 94, 98, 99, 102

Unique Properties, 62

****

Appendix 1

A landlord checklist of things to do before tenants move in

- ➢ Check tenants have the 'Right to Rent' Landlords must ensure tenants can legally reside in the UK before letting to them. The penalties for renting to someone without the right to rent from 2024 are set out below:

Per occupier (rented accommodation) first breach £10,000 repeat breach £20,000. Per lodger (private household) first breach £5,000 repeat breach £10,000. These rules are applicable from 2024.

- ➢ The government has issued a list of commonly available documents to check. If your tenants have the right to rent, take a copy of the document and keep it on file.
- ➢ Protect the deposit. Deposit protection is a legal requirement for landlords. Landlords must protect deposits within 30 days of receiving funds or face a fine of up to three times the deposit amount.
- ➢ Make your property fire safe. A smoke alarm must be on all floors of the property, and carbon monoxide detectors must be in any rooms with fuel-burning devices. If your property comes with furniture, it should be flame resistant.

- Make sure your Gas Safety Certificate is up to date If there's a gas supply at the property, you must arrange a gas safety inspection each year. You must give a copy of the certificate to tenants at the start of a tenancy.
- Make sure your EPC is up to date Landlords must have a valid EPC (Energy Performance Certificate) to let a property legally in the UK.
- You must give a copy of the certificate to tenants at the start of a tenancy.
- Give tenants a copy of the 'How to Rent' guide This guide lists landlord obligations and tenants' rights. You must either give
- tenants a hard copy or email it to them as an attachment. A
- link to the guide is not enough. Landlords who fail to do this are unable to evict tenants under a Section 21 Notice.
- Make sure appliances are in working order Any appliance left in the property must be safe to use. Anything not working should be replaced or removed.

You should also:
- Reference your tenants. This is the best insight into your tenant's ability to pay their rent on time. A good referencing service will check affordability, employability, credit history, and a previous landlord reference.

- Prepare an inventory. Although not a legal requirement, an inventory is vital for getting funds from the deposit. If tenants disagree with your deductions, you won't be able to claim anything without a signed inventory.
- Take meter readings. This keeps things fair. It means tenants will know what they're responsible to pay and helps prevent landlords from being left with outstanding payments.
- Update utility suppliers. It's a good idea to update utility suppliers with new tenant details.
- This ensures any utilities tenants use will be billed to them.
- Provide emergency contact numbers Important — especially for minimizing any damage caused to the property.
- If a pipe bursts in the middle of the night, for example, your tenants need to know who to call.
- Change the locks. Some might view this as an additional expense, but it could be essential for the safety of your new tenants. If you don't change the locks, you must be confident your previous tenants were trustworthy enough to return all copies of the keys.

****